EXORCISING TERROR

The Incredible Unending Trial of General Augusto Pinochet

Ariel Dorfman

AN OPEN MEDIA BOOK

SEVEN STORIES PRESS / NEW YORK

CONTENTS

DEDICATION 7

PROLOGUE 11

Exorcising Terror 17

FIRST EPILOGUE
The Shadow of Chile 193

SECOND EPILOGUE
The Long Good-Bye to Tyrants 195

Some Final Words in the Guise of an Acknowledgment 208

NOTES 212

FURTHER READING 214

ABOUT THE AUTHOR 217

ABOUT SEVEN STORIES PRESS 219

ABOUT OPEN MEDIA PAMPHLETS AND BOOKS 220

ALSO BY ARIEL DORFMAN 222

DEDICATION

*IF YOU VISIT THE Cementerio General in Santiago, Chile,
you will find, to one side and hugging its outskirts, a
large, extended granite memorial, a Wall of Memory
erected there in February of 1994, a few years after
democracy returned to my country. A number—more
than four thousand—of names have been chiseled into
its surface, all of them victims of the security forces of
General Augusto Pinochet during his dictatorship,
which lasted from September 11, 1973, until March 11,
1990. Next to the names of 1,002 men and women on
that wall no date of death has been engraved: These are
the desaparecidos, the disappeared, whose families have
not yet been able to bury them. Nor is the surface of the
wall entirely full: The sculptor and architects left an
enormous swath of stone to one side with no inscriptions. They anticipated that space would be needed for
new casualties to be written down and, in fact, slowly
and hesitantly, other families—now that they no longer
fear reprisals—have decided to announce the execution
or disappearance of their loved ones. When I visited a
Mapuche village in the faraway foothills of southern*

Chile some years ago, the elders told me that they would not report many of those who were massacred during the dictatorship for fear that the soldiers would someday come back and wreak vengeance. The wall will never contain all the names still hidden in the mists of fear and forgetfulness.

This book is dedicated to five friends whose names are on that wall in our cemetery in Santiago:

Freddy Taberna, who was executed by a military firing squad in Pisagua on October 30, 1973. His body was never returned to his family for burial.

Diana Aron, who was shot and wounded by the Chilean secret police on November 18, 1974, and taken to the torture house of Villa Grimaldi in Nuñoa. Her body has still not been recovered.

Fernando Ortiz, who was arrested on December 15, 1976, at Plaza Egaña in Santiago by members of the Chilean secret police in the presence of numerous witnesses. The authorities denied having him in custody. In 2001, information was released by the military indicating that his remains might be buried somewhere in a forsaken and desolate range of hills known as the Cuesta Barriga in central Chile. The bones that were discovered there, after months of false leads and hard digging, proved, through DNA testing, to belong to the man who had once been Fernando Ortiz.

Rodrigo Rojas Denegri, who on July 2, 1986, was burnt alive by a squad of soldiers and then transported to the other side of Santiago and left for dead in a ditch.

Ariel Dorfman

Four days later—at the age of nineteen—he died of his wounds in a Santiago hospital.

And Claudio Jimeno, who was arrested at the presidential palace of La Moneda in Santiago on September 11, 1973. For almost thirty years he had been missing, and then news from Santiago confirmed that his body, along with the bodies of several other advisers to former President Salvador Allende, had been dynamited the day after the coup, blown to bits so that no one would ever be able to find it or prove the tortures that had been inflicted upon it. Excavations in a military fort by an investigating judge led to the discovery of fragments of a bone that, identified as Claudio's, will now, apparently, allow him to be buried.

But this dedication, like the wall itself, like this book, can never really be complete.

Not if we remember this: The Chilean memorial does not include the names of those who lost their jobs and their homes and their health insurance and their pensions after the 1973 coup, a number estimated to be over a million. It does not include the men from the shantytowns who, night after night, were rounded up by patrols and beaten and made to stand at attention, naked, in a soccer field while beyond the glaring spotlights their wives and mothers and children were forced to watch. Nor do the names on the wall include almost a million exiles or migrants—close to one tenth of Chile's population at the time of the military takeover.

And the wall cannot, of course, include this memory

that was told to me by someone, a man who asked me many years ago not to reveal his name if I ever told his story:

"I was taken down into that basement, stumbling because of the tape over my eyes, taped like a second skin to my skin. Those hands scratched me as they tore the clothes, You son of a bitch, now you'll see what we do to bitches like you. Their fingernails were dirty, it was crazy that I should be worrying about getting an infection from those dirty fingernails, I had spent the last two weeks with hardly any food, unable to relieve myself, I was filthy and must have smelled worse than the worst sewer, but I nevertheless couldn't keep my mind off those fingernails, afraid that they would give me some sort of sickness. That was before they strapped me to the cot, one hand and then the other one, and someone else was binding my ankles, spreading me out under what must have been a blazing lightbulb. And then they attached something—a wire, a clasp, what was it?—they attached it to my genitals and then that voice said, Let's make him dance, let's make him sing, let's fuck him over. And then they made me dance. And they made me sing."

No, the wall does not include hundreds of thousands who were tortured and who survived, it does not include their memories.

Ariel Dorfman

PROLOGUE

DURING THE 1973 COUP, Chile's new military leaders, finding themselves with an excess of political prisoners on their hands, hit upon what must have seemed like an ingenious idea: Turn the National Stadium, our largest sports arena, into a gigantic concentration camp. Then, a few months later, after thousands of dissidents had been arrested and tortured, after hundreds had been interrogated and executed, the authorities scrubbed the floors and painted the benches and reopened the coliseum to the public. The referees again blew their whistles, the ball once again thudded across the field...and gradually soccer fans began coming back.

Ten years after the coup d'état, when I was allowed back from exile, finally allowed back to Chile, one of the decisions I made was not to visit that stadium, and for the next seven years, living in my country at times and at other times visiting it, I kept that vow. It was only when democracy returned that I was also able to return myself to that place where I had watched so many sports events in democratic times. What I had desperately needed was to witness some sort of act that would transform the stadium, that would reject its purported normality as obscene and confront the terrible pain still echoing there, and on March 12, 1990, the day after Pinochet gave up the presidency to Patricio Aylwin, the people of Chile performed that act of exorcism against the backdrop of the majestic Andes. Seventy thousand supporters gathered in the stadium to listen to the new democratic president in his first official encounter with the renewed land—and Aylwin did not let us down. In his speech he referred to the horrors that had happened in these stands and on this field and pledged "*nunca más*," never again. Far more pivotal than his words, however, in ridding the stadium of its demons, was the communal act of mourning that preceded them.

Seventy thousand men and women suddenly hushed as they heard a solitary pianist playing, down on the green field, variations on a song by Victor Jara, the celebrated protest singer murdered by the military a few days after the coup. As the melody died, a group of women in black skirts and white blouses emerged, carrying placards with photos of their *desaparecidos*. And then one of the women—a wife, a daughter, a mother?—began to dance a *cueca*, our national dance, dancing all her immense solitude because she was dancing alone a dance meant for a couple. There was a moment of shocked silence followed by the sound of people, slowly, tentatively, starting to clap along with the music, a savage, tender beating of palms that said to the nearby watching mountains that

Ariel Dorfman

sharing that sorrow, that we were also dancing with all our missing loves of history, all our dead, and that we were bringing them back somehow from the invisibility to which Pinochet had banished them. And as if answering us from beyond time, the Symphony Orchestra of Chile burst out with the chorale from Beethoven's Ninth Symphony and the song adopted by the Chilean resistance in its street battles, Schiller's Ode to Joy, his prophecy of a day "when all men will once again be brothers."

I had never seen before—and would never want to see again—seventy thousand people crying together as they lay their dead to rest. And yet, that unspoken and painful task was the one we set ourselves that day: to repeatedly liberate, in the years to come, all the zones, one after the other, that Pinochet had invaded.

It turned out to be a task that we would be unable to accomplish by ourselves.

It turned out to be a task that would require a little help from our friends.

David Burnett captured this image of a young man being arrested in the cellars of the national stadium a few days after the coup. It took David over twenty-five years to find that the man had not been killed, but survived. For all that time, the prisoner had not wanted to reveal his name out of fear.

EXORCISING
TERROR

"HAVE YOU HEARD about Pinochet?"

Oh, my God. Not him again. Not Pinochet. Not this early in the morning. Not ever. Pinochet? Pinochet? I was sick of Pinochet.

"Pinochet?"

I couldn't stop myself. I pronounced those dreaded syllables. Maybe Victoria Sanford—a graduate student who had volunteered to come and pick me up at my Berkeley hotel so I could catch a pre-dawn plane on that October 17 of 1998—would not add yet another hideous bit of news to the dismal string of tidings always associated with that name, the sort I had been receiving for the last twenty-five years.

Instead, Victoria shocked me with something absolutely unexpected: "He's been arrested in London," she said. "Last night. Scotland Yard, acting on an order from a Spanish judge."

I thought to myself, my mind automatically switching into the Spanish I bizarrely shared with General Pinochet: *Esto tiene que ser un sueño.* This has to be a dream. Which had been Victoria's reaction, she told me as we headed for the San Francisco airport across the Bay, when she had awoken that morning—the detention of the former Chilean dictator could not possibly be true. But the radio had repeated the news a second time, as if the announcer himself wasn't able to believe it: The night before, the police had, in fact, surrounded the London Clinic where Pinochet was recovering from a back operation, and then a squad had gone in to inform him he was being detained to await extradition hearings by order of Judge Baltasar Garzón—on charges of genocide, no less.

One hour later, as my plane took off, I still knew no more than those meager details. I was up in the air—in more than one sense. I recalled something that had happened to a friend, a Chilean like me, on the afternoon of September 11, 1973. He was in Paris and had just boarded a train for Rome—the Palatino, an express that made no stops on the way—and, as the doors shut, he had caught a glimpse of the latest edition of *Le Monde* in someone's hands, there, down on the platform. COUP D'ÈTAT AU CHILI. "Military takeover in Chile," the headlines screamed at him. And kept screaming at him and within him for the infinite hours of the night it took the train to cross Europe, without my friend being able to descend or find out what had happened to his country, his family, his friends, his president. Trapped inside the news. Who was alive, who was dead, what would happen to us? Not knowing that at about the time the doors were hissing together in France, on the other side of the planet, way down in the Southern Hemisphere, in our country that hugs the Pacific Ocean like a dagger pointing at the heart of Antarctica, as Kissinger once said—how could my friend guess that I was asking myself those same questions along with millions of our compatriots, huddled in front of a radio listening to a voice we would come to identify in the days and months and years to come, the gruff, nasal twanging bark of General Augusto Pinochet announcing the first decree of the military junta: Whoever was caught on the streets during curfew would immediately be shot.

Most Chileans had never before heard the voice that would henceforth accompany every moment of their private and public lives.

In my case, however, as an unofficial adviser to Fernando Flores, Salvador Allende's chief of staff, I spent all my days and many of my nights at La Moneda, the colonial building in the capital of Santiago that houses the executive branch and that's where, one afternoon in August 1973, the phone rang and, on the other end of the line, I heard the rasping growl of "El General Augusto Pinochet Ugarte," as he impatiently identified himself. During the tense waning weeks of Chile's experiment in creating socialism through peaceful means, Pinochet was known as the most loyal of all the military to the democratic regime. I rapidly passed him on to Flores— deaf to what that voice of Pinochet was hiding, the betrayal he was devising, the coup that had already happened in his mind.

That was it: no more than a fleeting phone conversation. But I spent the years that followed brooding over the other phone calls the General must have made in the days that were to come: the call ordering the air force to bomb the presidential palace, where Allende died; the call disbanding the Chilean Congress; the call to arrest Orlando Letelier and the call to mutilate and execute Enrique París and the call to disappear Carlos Berger and the call to cut the throat of José Manuel Parada and the call to burn Carmen Gloria Quintana alive.

I would register it all from exile, from Buenos Aires and Paris, from Amsterdam and Washington, carefully, almost perversely, almost as if I were punishing myself for not having recognized what the future was brewing for us, for my ineffectiveness at predicting what the hands that had dialed that number at La Moneda had in store for me and my adopted homeland. Yes, he was the one. Even if I knew that there were so many others to blame, that these crimes could only have been committed with thousands of others helping and millions standing by indifferently. It was Pinochet, always Pinochet. When I read in a human rights report that 180,000 people had been summarily detained in the first year of the dictatorship, an estimated 90 percent of them tortured. And when I greeted my friend Oscar Castro in France, expelled from Chile after a two-year term in a prison camp for having staged a play about the captain of a sinking ship who whispers to his crew to stay alive and continue the struggle, when I had to console him for his mother's disappearance at the hands of the secret police. And when I would read in one paper and another that 27 percent of Chile's population was receiving 3.3 percent of the country's income and would try to conjure from these dry statistics the faces of the poor, the families I had worked with for years in the Santiago shantytowns and how they had to eat cats in order to survive. And when a letter informed me of the child prostitutes that now beggared the city. It was Pinochet, *ese hijo de puta Pinochet*, who was responsible, always Pinochet who stood between me and the land I was not allowed to return to, between all of us and the normal lives we could no longer live while he was in power. And yet, for all the satanic dimensions I attributed to his hands and his voice, at the same time he remained, for me, strangely ethereal, almost disembodied.

I scanned his past and newspaper clippings to discover traces of the man who controlled Chile—the man who could offhandedly remark that not a leaf fell anywhere in the country without his knowing about it. I looked for clues and found next to nothing, hardly an anticipation. As I pored over his autobiography—his carefree childhood in the 1920s at the port of Valparaíso, his pranks as a military cadet in the 1930s, his three undistinguished books on geopolitics where not a controversial statement or political position of any sort could be garnered, his lumbering, nondescript military career—I could not dispel the sense that he was hiding, that he had been hiding perhaps even from his own self all his life, learning from an early age not to tell anybody who he really was, perhaps not even revealing to his own mirror or wife the person he could someday become.

There was, in the entire haystack of his past, only one intriguing incident. Back in 1946, President Gabriel González Videla, already choosing the side of the United States in the burgeoning Cold War, had expelled from his government the Communists who, as part of the Popular Front Coalition, had helped to elect him. González Videla rounded up thousands of his former allies and dispatched them to a concentration camp opened in the northern desert region, just outside the isolated, run-down port of Pisagua. In charge of this facility was the man who, almost thirty years later, would reopen Pisagua yet one more time to ship his own enemies there: Captain Augusto Pinochet. And it was in Pisagua, on a day in 1947, that Pinochet was to have his first encounter with another man from Valparaíso, Salvador Allende, who, as a *diputado* (member of Congress) from the Socialist Party, was heading a congressional delegation that had come to investigate the conditions under which the prisoners were being held. When Allende, stopped by the military, had announced that he would complete his visit with or without permission, Pinochet had answered with threats to shoot him if he tried. According to Pinochet's memoir, the man who was someday to become president of Chile had backed down.

Later on, the General was to worry that this violent confrontation would come back to haunt him, but Allende never again alluded to it, and certainly did not remember it when he designated Pinochet Commander in Chief of the Army on August 23, 1973, just nineteen days before the coup. So crafty Pinochet had fooled the savvy President and just about everybody else, swearing in a letter to Allende—written at about the time I had picked up the phone and initially heard his gruff voice—that he would give his life to defend the president and the constitution. And Pinochet had not, in fact, joined the conspiracy to overthrow the man who had named him to his post until the last moment, but once he had taken the plunge, *el General* went about systematically eliminating or subordinating every rival and ally. This seemed to be his central characteristic: an unceasing, almost lethal, ability to dupe his enemies. Deep cunning cloaked under a mantle of gray invisibility. *Cazurro* is the word we use in Spanish. Hiding all his life and still hiding as I tried so many years later to pin him down from my banishment. Slipping away. Only corporeal for me in those three brief, innocent seconds when I had registered his voice over the phone. Pinochet was everything in my life. And yet, he was also nothing.

But someday...someday this would change, I told myself, we all told ourselves, inside and outside Chile. Someday, I would return victoriously to my homeland and we would be given the satisfaction of watching Pinochet tried for his crimes, hearing that voice imploring forgiveness, we would witness those hands humiliated and handcuffed. Though it turned out that I was the one who, in 1983, had to return with my hands behind my back to a country where Pinochet was still very much in control. Nor did my return bring him any closer. The General lived behind an imposing wall of security, at a distance from Chile—as I had lived for the ten years of my exile. Nobody I knew had ever caught more than a glimpse of him. Even in Santiago, he continued to be everything and nothing.

It was one evening during that first visit home after exile, as I was returning to uptown Santiago from one of the city's miserable suburbs, that I finally saw General Pinochet for the first time—or saw at least part of him. I had spent most of the afternoon with a group of destitute youngsters who spoke of their addiction to benzene fumes, the cheapest, quickest escape from an infernal reality. They told me of brutal police raids and the lack of jobs in a zone where the unemployment rate was, according to a priest who ministered to the boys and their families, verging on 70 percent.

My then brother-in-law, the filmmaker Ignacio Agüero, had driven me to that slum, and on our way back, at the exact intersection of Antonio Varas and Eleodoro Yáñez streets, our car was brought to a halt by a screeching siren and a hive of braking motorcycles. "It's Pinochet, it's Pinochet," Ignacio murmured anxiously. A caravan of black cars raced by, and just as it passed us, a white-gloved hand darted out of one of the windows and waved, in the typical gesticulation of dignitaries acknowledging a cheering crowd. It was absurd: There was nobody there except us.

And then he was gone. An apparition.

Pinochet, of course, had no idea that I was watching him. And yet I felt that the General was mocking me—

Ariel Dorfman

that his ghostly hand in the dusk was gesturing defiantly: I am here to stay, this is as near as you and your kind will ever get to me, this is the only farewell you will ever see from me. I am as far from justice as I am from your hungry eyes.

That incident turned out to be, in some vexing way, prophetic of what was to come. He was protected, I came to feel, by those phantasmagoric gloves, dismissively eluding even the idea that he could be judged. Insulated from any possible accountability, those hands of his had signed into law an amnesty for himself and his men in 1978, and even after he lost a plebiscite ten years later and was reluctantly forced out of office in 1990, that voice I had first heard so many years earlier kept on threatening another coup if anybody in the new democratic Chile dared touch him, in fact staging two revolts to make sure that not one of his officers would ever be so much as called to testify—though he had also extracted from the authorities a promise that they would quash an investigation into the corrupt business deals that had turned Pinochet's oafish son into a multimillionaire. No idle threats from the former dictator—who for the first eight years of the return to democracy stayed on as Commander in Chief of the Army. And when he left the army in March 1998, arrogant as ever, and became Senator for Life, he continued to dictate policy and warn his enemies not to move against him or his associates, while the Supreme Court packed with his own designated judges refused to consider any accusations of human rights violations. As all this happened, I told myself—now from afar, an expatriate who had decided not to return to Chile—that he would mock us forever, that we would never be rid of his person or his legacy. Those hands shrouded in white would go to the grave without once having had to confront what they had done, what they had made other hands do.

And yet, it now seemed that history had other plans for the wrists and fingers of General Pinochet. Other hands, the hands of English policemen, had stormed into his life and ours; the hands of a Spanish judge had the tyrant cornered.

Perhaps my fractured visions of him through these years—the disembodied voice; those faded newspaper clippings; the fragments of a life in hiding; the white, white glove—were, after all, prescient, intimations of a possible farewell. Was I finally going to get the chance, was my country about to be allowed, to wave good-bye to General Augusto Pinochet?

· · · · ·

Believe me, General: Your detention in London is the best thing that could have happened to you.

I understand that it can't be pleasant to find yourself arrested without warning, not to be able to amble along the streets of Chelsea whenever you feel like it, not to know what future awaits you. Just ask the many Chileans who, after your men came for them in the mid-

Ariel Dorfman

dle of the night, were not exactly lodged in five-star London clinics.

But if you're scared, and you feel alone, and you think you've been stabbed in the back, perhaps you should consider that destiny may have offered you at the very end of your life a providential chance to save your soul. You have, for the last twenty-five years, been living an illusion, constructing a sham version of yourself, obsessively justifying it. Knowing that you betrayed Salvador Allende, the man to whom you swore eternal loyalty.

That first act of treachery was followed by others, an inevitable avalanche of betrayals. The first great crime always needs to be covered up with more crimes. Dictators aspire to total power in order to seek refuge from the demons they have unchained. As a way of silencing their ghosts, they demand to be surrounded by a rampart of flattering mirrors and genuflecting counselors that assure the tyrant that yes, you are the most beautiful of them all, the best, the one who knows more.

And you ended up believing them, General.

You defended yourself from what you had done, what you were doing, with the isolating walls of your supposed invulnerability, the conviction that nobody would ever hold you accountable, that there was one law for you and a different law for the rest of your compatriots. And even when the people of Chile forced you to accept democracy and leave power, you were still able, with an uncanny instinct, to trap the whole country in a transition where you would never have to answer for even one *of your deeds or your words, a transition where you were the only one who was really free to say and do what you wanted whenever you wanted to, while your fellow countrymen always had to be careful of their mouths, careful even of our thoughts.*

We couldn't, given the terms of the transaction we agreed to under the specter of your guns, express our true emotions, fearful that if you didn't like our latest move you would just up and kick the table on which the game was being played, shoot the player who had dared to trump your card. We got our democracy back, General, but you set the limits of how far and deep that democracy could go.

And then you confused your country with the world. You thought you could travel to England, a nation that symbolized civility and civilization to you. You thought you could walk along the Thames as if it were the Mapocho. You thought that the English would respect the rules and compacts of Chile, would be as subservient as Chile. You thought that sipping tea with Margaret Thatcher would protect you.

It is doubly sweet to think that you ensnared yourself, General, that it was the same hubris with which you governed that ended up blinding you, befuddling your sense of reality, lulling you into the fantasy that you could always impose your will upon everybody else, making sure you would never have to look at the nearby pain you had caused other human beings.

I want you to know, General, that I don't believe in

Ariel Dorfman

the death penalty. What I do believe in is human redemption. Even yours, General Augusto Pinochet. That's why, for the last twenty-five years, I've wanted so much for this to come to pass: that at least once before your death those eyes of yours would have to look at the black and clear eyes of the women whose sons and husbands and fathers and brothers you kidnapped and disappeared, one woman and then another woman and then one more.

I wanted them to have the opportunity to tell you how their lives were splintered and ravaged by an order you gave or an order you never blocked. I am about to find out what would happen if you were required to listen day after day to the numberless stories of your victims. If you were forced to recognize their existence.

You believe in God, General, a comfort I have not permitted myself, but you may, therefore, be able to decipher what your wise and compassionate and severe Lord has sent you as your life draws to a close: the chance to repent. To penetrate into the fierce circle of your crimes and ask forgiveness. Do you know something, Don Augusto? Personally, as far as I am concerned, that would be enough. It would be punishment enough. And think of what a great contribution it would be to the country you say you love, you say you did all this for: You could help our shared motherland take one more step in the arduous, tentative task of reconciliation, which is only possible if the terrible truth of what has been done to us is revealed and acknowledged, if you *participate in this bruising search for the truth without lying to us or yourself.*

Remember what history and religion and also literature—think of Dostoevski, yes, even if he is a Russian!—teach us: The best thing that can happen to a criminal is to be captured, because in his solitary cell, without the habitual defenses with which he has hidden his past from himself, at times the miracle of a minute window opens inside the prisoner's heart, a window that might lead to self-awareness and redemption.

I am aware, of course, that it is not likely that you will use this occasion to act like a genuinely free man, someone who can forswear his fear and decipher the enigma of his life, can suddenly see himself as the immense majority of humanity sees him, can understand why we want to purge you from our existence. Purge you and so many other despots of this genocidal century.

Aunque nunca es demasiado tarde, General.

It's never too late, General.

• • • • •

There was a moment, during that morning of September 11, 1973, when President Salvador Allende must have realized he was going to die. Yes, there are more Septembers of terror in history than most people remember; yes, there exists another Tuesday, the eleventh of September, when death also descended from the sky: The bombs and missiles were falling from the Hawker Hunters that day in Santiago, the leaders of the coup had rallied the armed forces behind them and were already exterminating civilians, an ultimatum had been delivered.

Allende convoked his hundred or so associates, those who, up till then, had been fighting by his side, and he demanded that all the women present, along with any man who didn't know how to use a weapon, immediately leave the presidential palace. Among those saved by the president were his own pregnant daughter Beatriz and a twenty-nine-year-old Catalán lawyer, Joan Garcés, who had become Allende's political adviser and his confidant over the last three years of democratic socialist government. Garcés was smuggled out of Chile by the Spanish Embassy and as his plane left the country that had attempted a revolution without blood, he swore he would not forget the dead president or the other victims of that military takeover.

Years later, the son of Augusto Pinochet—the very one who had accumulated all those millions during his loving papa's reign—complained that his father should have driven a stake through the heart of Joan Garcés rather than letting him escape abroad.

For once, Pinochet's son was right.

During the decades that followed, without neglecting his work as a lawyer and later, as a parliamentarian in his Spanish homeland, Garcés always clung to the belief that it was possible to put General Pinochet on trial for his crimes. He created a foundation named after Salvador

Allende; filled several rooms at his office and home with stacks of files and information; and, at the head of Progressive Lawyers, an association he helped to establish, led a campaign to make foreign dictators accountable in the Spanish courts. What seemed at first a quixotic endeavor began to appear more legally viable as Spain signed a series of treaties, in particular the European Convention on Torture. And when it became evident that the rulers of newly democratic Chile were unable or unwilling to bring Pinochet to justice, the relatives of those executed and disappeared turned to Joan Garcés, the man who had spent countless hours listening to their stories, their depositions, their accusations. Perhaps Garcés and his colleagues would be able to exact some measure of retribution.

On July 5, 1996, the Audiencia Nacional, Spain's Superior Court, accepted the right of a group of lawyers to present in the court of Valencia an accusation against General Augusto Pinochet and other members of the Junta for the death and disappearance of Spanish citizens in Chile. It was to be the first of many other criminal proceedings brought against Pinochet: Chilean victims were subsequently added to the growing dossier.

These efforts did not immediately bear any visible fruit—except to make Pinochet wary of entering Spain, misgivings he did not have regarding England, a country he visited frequently to cement the acquisition of arms for the Chilean military, business deals that included, it has been suggested, fat commissions for himself and his family. And, as he was invariably received in London and elsewhere with all the honors and privileges his rank and diplomatic passport commanded, Pinochet never seemed overly worried by these exertions by his enemies abroad.

And I thought he was right. I can, in fact, uncertainly remember one morning—it must have been sometime in the mid-nineties—when I received a breathless call from my Dutch friend Max Arian.

"We almost got him."

"Who?"

"Pinochet. We found out he was staying here, in Amsterdam, at the Amstel Hotel—and Amnesty International convinced a judge to serve a warrant for his arrest. But he was warned and left before anything could happen. At least we made him leave hastily, we made him sweat."

That seemed to be the limit of these pursuits: to make him sweat. An idealistic, almost chimerical quest, I thought to myself, like so many crusades in the world today fought by starry-eyed utopians battling for lost causes. Even as I admired their tenacity, their refusal to give up, I did not doubt that they were deluding themselves.

And perhaps history would have confirmed my pessimism, if the mission Garcés had set himself had not been seconded by another Spaniard, whose last name, strangely enough, also started with the same letters, G-A-R. Baltasar Garzón had made a name for himself as the youngest judge at the Audiencia Nacional, fearlessly prosecuting drug traffickers, the officials of the Basque separatist organization, ETA, and later on, the members of the Socialist government who had created illegal squads to torture and eliminate the ETA terrorists. Since 1996, Garzón had been investigating the death of Spanish citizens during the Argentine military dictatorship and had demanded the extradition of the Argentine officers involved in those crimes. In mid-1998, Garzón took over the cases Garcés had been filing and that another judge had been working on.

And when these two men—the lawyer who had brought the accusation and the judge who was trying to determine the merits of that accusation—were alerted by Amnesty International to the fact that Pinochet had gone into a London clinic for a back operation on October 8 and would be immobilized for the next ten days, unable to escape—as he had done when the Dutch had attempted to capture him—they made their move.

Working secretly and with great haste, Garzón issued an international warrant for the arrest of one Augusto Pinochet Ugarte, a fugitive from justice, and sent the order of apprehension to Interpol.

It was a race against time. The great crusading journalist Hugh O'Shaughnessy had published an article in the *London Guardian* on October 15 denouncing the General's presence in England and hoping that this man who had tortured British surgeon Sheila Cassidy and killed so many others would be arrested. When the Chilean Embassy had asked the Foreign Office if any action was pending, apparently the British concealed what was about to happen and answered that it had no information to that effect. Alarmed, nevertheless, people in Pinochet's retinue were planning to decamp with the ailing former dictator on October 17.

They were too late. The night before their flight, at around 9:00 PM, the English magistrate Nicholas Evans, at home after a long day's work, agreed to sign the arrest warrant. A few hours later, exactly at 11:25, detectives from Scotland Yard stormed into the clinic and informed the man who had made the mistake of not killing Joan Garcés that he was under arrest. They read General Augusto Pinochet his rights and let him know that Judge Baltasar Garzón was waiting in Madrid to put him on trial for genocide and crimes against humanity.

●　●　●　●　●

So now I have been awakening every morning before dawn. At 4:48, to be precise. Ever since Pinochet's arrest, to be even more precise—since that first dawn in Berkeley. I can't help it, my eyes automatically snap open at that insane hour and I switch on the radio here in the silence of my house in North Carolina and, trying to dodge the unpublishable imprecations of my wife, Angélica, I listen anxiously to the BBC newscast on our local station—ten o'clock in the morning, London time. Some compulsive inner watch demands that I tune in to the latest developments, I have to know *immediately* if something new has happened to the dictator, what recent clue may have just surfaced about his ultimate destiny.

In spite of my hurry, I am aware that it will not be easy and it will not go quickly, this trial of General Pinochet. The man is being afforded, as he should be, each and every one of the rights he denied to his victims. Nobody will rape his daughters to extract a confession from him or gouge out his eyes to make sure he cannot identify his jailers or hang him from his thumbs for fifty days and nights until he pleads for mercy or tape his mouth and knock out his teeth so he cannot speak out in his own defense. He will not be refused counsel, his relatives will not be lied to about his whereabouts, medical attention will not be withheld.

I cannot argue with this: The General, like every human being born on this earth, should be presumed innocent until proven guilty. Which means, in practical terms, an excruciatingly endless series of judicial proceedings. As in any case where the defendant has the resources to pay for the best lawyers, the road ahead is fraught with petitions and writs and hearings and statutory wrangling. Each day has brought and will bring yet again a fresh assault on the case for extraditing the General: In fact, the hasty provisional warrant that led to Pinochet's arrest on October 16 turned out to be insufficient, as it only mentioned Spanish citizens murdered during the first decade of the dictatorship, and was impugned by the Chilean government on October 17 as not constituting an extradition crime in England; it was therefore followed by a second warrant issued by Garzón on October 18, carefully tailored to English law, one that recognizes torture as an offense wherever the act of torture may have been committed, which resulted in Pinochet's re-arrest on October 22 on new charges of genocide and terrorism.

This new warrant has also been challenged by Pinochet's lawyers and there is now a writ of habeas corpus and a petition for dismissal being argued at a Divisional Court (also known as the High Court). Whatever those three justices may decide, what awaits those of us who are watching seems interminable: requests for judicial review and requests for the revision of the review, appeals and counterappeals, all of which will snake ever farther up the judicial ladder of England, all the way to the Law Lords who sit in the House of Lords as a British equivalent of the Supreme Courts of other lands. Indeed, the never-ending suit will probably end up there in front of them who knows how many times more before this is over, that is, if the home secretary does not decide to intervene at his discretion and send the eighty-two-year-old Chilean General packing home, an eventual decision that does not yet seem forthcoming but that, if it were to materialize, could also, according to some, be contested legally by the Crown prosecution service acting on behalf of the Spanish judge.

In spite of the exhausting juridical intricacies, Pinochet's trial, even in its preliminary stages—which merely seek to determine the lawfulness of his arrest—is no ordinary case. Its outcome could determine for decades to come a whole range of crucial legal and human rights issues. Even before the question of the General's specific innocence or guilt comes up, other matters need to be resolved. Can a former head of state be tried for crimes allegedly committed during his regime? Does the amnesty prevalent in his homeland—or the immunity extended to him by the laws of that homeland—apply to a foreign nation? Can an English court—or a Spanish court, for that matter—consider indictments dealing with transgressions perpetrated in Chile, even if they do not include English or Spanish nationals? When do international laws supersede national law? And what might be the consequences for national sovereignty of conceding to tribunals outside one's land the right to judge crimes committed at home? Do smaller countries need to fear that this sort of action against Pinochet, if condoned, will be a weapon of the strong against them? Or will stronger nations understand this kind of trial as a threat to their own leaders and military personnel, who could presumably be arrested in the future due to alleged (and often all-too-real) interventions that they ordered or carried out in foreign lands?

How does this upcoming trial of Pinochet affect the international tribunals that are being set up to deal with the atrocities that have recently occurred in the Balkans and Rwanda and in previous decades in Cambodia and Ethiopia? How will it alter the different legal actions being brought against other dictators living out their

Ariel Dorfman

golden exile on the funds they stole from their people, dictators like Hebré in Senegal, Duvalier in France, Idi Amin in Saudi Arabia, Stroessner in Brazil, Mengistu in Zimbabwe? What about Salvadoran death squad commanders García and Vides Casanova, who have been granted refuge in the United States and are contentedly bathing in Florida waters while thousands of Central American and Caribbean refugees are turned away? Will it change anything in Cuba, where Fidel Castro—Pinochet's biggest enemy—has paradoxically voiced aloud his preoccupation at this assault upon the immunity of heads of state and has reportedly enjoined his personal guard to fight to the death if any such attempt is made against him when he travels abroad? Will the Pinochet affair make current strongmen who might contemplate an early retirement (like Mobutu or Milosevic) more reluctant to withdraw from power and fight on to the end—in a place like, say, Liberia or Indonesia or Iraq, if safety in eventual havens abroad can no longer be guaranteed?

To summarize: At a time when everything has been globalized, from capital to communications to production, what about justice, what about its globalization? In an age when humanity is being redefined and unified across frontiers, who speaks in humanity's name, who judges and punishes in the name of that humanity?

No wonder that this trial may take years. With stakes that high....

The players are not only the General and his panoply

of extravagantly paid lawyers in one corner (Pinochet can afford it, if there is any truth to what journalists have written about the money he's made from his family's involvement with drug trafficking), and in the other the British prosecution acting on behalf of a Spanish judge and countless victims. A number of other actors, some visible, some lurking in the shadows, are trying to sway and manipulate the proceedings: Professing to respect the judiciary and its autonomy, these others are aware that justice never operates in a vacuum and that less conspicuous factors, from diplomacy to public opinion, may ultimately determine this case's denouement.

Besides the three countries directly involved in this process (England, where the General is being held; Spain, where the indictment originated; and, of course, poor Chile), other nations are entering the fray. Prosecutors in France and Belgium, Holland and Germany, Switzerland and Italy, are studying the possibility of issuing warrants for Pinochet's arrest for the murder of their own citizens during his reign, lining up to bring him to justice if the British are to release the former dictator. The United States has been keeping a prudent distance from the litigation so far, but its government would not be unhappy if the General were to find himself flying home on a Chilean military jet that has been dispatched to a nearby English airbase to await his possible freedom. It is not merely that the United States is worried about the precedent and spectacle of a former head of state (or any other high official) on trial in a foreign land for crimes against humanity—the name of Kissinger keeps cropping up insistently, as does that of George Bush Sr. and a series of assorted others who could be and have been accused internationally of promoting terror abroad. Compounding the worry for the Washington establishment is the fact that this is Chile, the country whose democracy the United States destabilized and helped to destroy.

Any trial of General Pinochet is bound to bring out even more unsavory details of that flagrant intervention. And reveal yet again the scandalous reluctance of the United States itself to press for Pinochet's extradition to face in a Washington court the charges that he ordered the murder of Allende's former minister of foreign affairs and Defense, Orlando Letelier, and his American aide, Ronni Moffit. It is only due to U.S. pressure that the man directly responsible for that covert operation, Manuel Contreras, the former head of the Chilean secret police, was sentenced in Santiago and is now serving a jail sentence in a luxury prison built specially to house him. What if similar demands were made to force the Chileans to cough up Pinochet? How would that trial—of a head of state who blew up two persons on the streets of the U.S. capital—play in the media, given that the main terrorist was installed in power by American intelligence agencies and American multinational corporations? But there is more: A major part of the Spanish indictment against Pinochet is based on how his secret service was instrumental in creating, with the aid of the CIA, a terrorist conspiracy known as

Operation Condor, which allowed Chile, Argentina, Bolivia, Brazil, Paraguay, and Uruguay to pursue, torture, and murder political opponents in each other's countries and in other lands during the 1970s. Not to mention the help that the Chilean military gave, through Operation Condor, to Anastasio Somoza, the Nicaraguan tyrant, before the Sandinistas chased him from power in 1979, and the support given by the Argentines, at U.S. instigation, to the death squads in El Salvador.[1] So I am not surprised at reports in the press that the Chilean government has enlisted its United States allies to apply diplomatic pressure on the British and the Spanish so that this case can be quickly resolved.

The British, for now, do not seem to be budging. This is a Labour government, and Jack Straw (the home secretary who must eventually make key decisions on whether to allow the extradition to proceed or to interrupt the hearings at some point because of the General's ill health and age) visited Chile during the Allende years as a young firebrand socialist to cheer on the revolution. The left wing of Labour, as well as much of the English press and the intelligentsia, are enjoying the humiliation of Pinochet and his dear pal, the Iron Lady, who has absurdly declared that the General should be congratulated for bringing democracy to Chile—which is about equivalent to declaring that free-marketeer Thatcher brought socialism to Great Britain.

In Spain, however, the conservative government of Premier José María Aznar is doing all it can to obstruct

Ariel Dorfman

and even sabotage Garzón's case. Aznar is concerned about the threats—some veiled and some quite dire—from Chilean businessmen against the huge Spanish economic interests in Chile. But the overwhelming antifascist popular sentiment in Spain—90 to 95 percent of those polled want to see Pinochet tried in Madrid, the Spanish doing to the Chilean admirer and disciple of Franco what they were unable to do to Franco himself—is keeping Aznar at bay. On the other hand, an election is looming in two years' time, and the worst nightmare for the conservatives would be to have Pinochet in the dock during the campaign, reminding the public every day of Aznar and company's roots in the fascist Catholic nationalism that gave birth to Pinochet and Franco, and that the right wing needs to keep out of sight if it is to win another term in office. So the Spanish government will try to discreetly block and weaken the extradition proceedings but has to be wary of not self-destructing along the way. Thus far, every contemptible effort of government justice officials to deny Garzón's jurisdiction in the case—or to stop him, for instance, from adding cases to the indictment—has been rebuffed over and over again by different tribunals in Madrid and denounced in the Spanish press.

This multiple chess game, played out on at least three continents and with more entanglements than I could list, gets even more convoluted if we add to the mix members of the international business brotherhood and their wealthy Chilean counterparts, all of them fabulously enriched by Pinochet's policy of selling off profit-making public enterprises to private speculators at ridiculously low prices while simultaneously opening the country to foreign predators. Anybody else? Diverse arms merchants and providers of tanks and planes and missiles and vessels who, lavishly rewarded by the General for the last two decades, are now also showing their loyalty.

On the other side, the cast is enlivened by two other international contestants. Of decisive importance is a coalition of human rights groups that have been struggling for years to bring people like Pinochet to justice and who regard this occasion as one where their resources, wisdom, and skills will be tested. Amnesty International, Human Rights Watch, and the Center for the Victims of Torture have asked to be part of the prosecution team and are frantically gathering information, holding press conferences. All these nongovernmental organizations are seconded by the surprise appearance of yet another major protagonist in this drama: the *Piquete de Londres*. Primarily from the European countries, though also from other parts of the world, hundreds (and, on occasion, thousands) of Chilean exiles have converged upon London to surround the different places where the conflict is evolving. They are there every morning when the lawyers and the judges arrive at the courthouse, banging drums, waving admonitory bilingual signs, engaging in street theater with masks and costumes and ritual ketchup on their white shirts, performing the General's misdeeds for the roving and ever-hungry televisual eye. Many of these protesters are themselves victims who never went home:

men and women who were jailed, beaten, banished, who dreamt of those hands of Pinochet as I did in the interminable years of their homelessness, and who have now had their foe delivered into their midst.

Perhaps more poignant, however, is the presence of many youngsters in the *Piquete*, the sons and daughters of those who were sent into exile over twenty years ago and who have suddenly rediscovered a Chilean identity corroded by time and distance. These bodies—born in and out of Chile, born before and after Allende—give a weight and reality to the accusations against Pinochet. And they are making his life miserable. He did not leave them alone and they are returning the favor. The very day after he was arrested, they were already outside the clinic, picketing and shouting and singing, and the drums, the drums, the drums, the noise reaching Pinochet in his secluded bed and forcing the managers of this venerable London medical facility to suggest that the General and his entourage decamp for other pastures. But the members of the *Piquete* have followed their enemy to his next location—a sort of high-scale resting home for the insane—and have continued making such a commotion that finally Pinochet, now derisively known as The English Patient, has had to rent, in the faraway outskirts of London, a house deep inside the grounds of a gated community, imprisoned as much by the vociferation of the protesters outside the portals as by the Scotland Yard policemen who incessantly watch him from closer by.

This is the place where I imagine him every morning as I wake. I like to think of him listening to the same program, think of him enclosed and unable to move from his quarters, the man who could have the lackeys around him obey the slightest motion of his little finger, that's all he needed, to lift his pinkie and someone could die, and now his eyes rise from the radio and see the green expanse of extremely British lawn outside the house and he suddenly knows what it means to be far from home in a foreign land where everything is strange and hostile and the hunters and the dead are at the gate.

It is an absurd reverie on my part: The General does not listen to the BBC and he most certainly doesn't understand a word of English and he is not haunted by any ghosts. But this is my way of telling myself that, even if he is to be freed soon by one or another court, nobody will ever take from us those instances of his unfathomable despair, the penalty already meted out to him extending far beyond anything we could have wildly conjectured a month ago.

So I awaken every dawn because of the joy it provides me, the sense that some slight balance has been restored to an imperfect and damaged universe where evil is so rarely punished.

But what if we lose?

Not a rhetorical question. Just now on the radio, I hear the news—today, October 28, 1998—that the English High Court has ruled, by three to zero, that Senator Pinochet, as a former head of state, has immunity, even if he killed people while president. Both Spanish arrest warrants are illegal and the extradition cannot therefore proceed.

The ruling, the radio announces, will be immediately appealed by Garzón's lawyers to the House of Lords. And I think to myself with dread that maybe this whole case is going to make dictators less accountable than ever, maybe it will set back the whole movement to ferret out these despots, maybe Pinochet will go down in history as the tyrant who got away.

• • • • •

It is not true, in fact, that this is the first time General Pinochet has been on trial. His current predicament is only possible because all these years we have been putting him on trial in the vast inner spaces of our hopes and dreams, Chileans and foreigners, never letting up in our accusations, ever since the coup asking him questions in our mind that we could not ask him in reality, biting our tongues and finally accepting the sad evidence that he could and would never be held accountable, that this was the price Chile had to pay in order to get our freedom back.

In my own case, I wanted this trial so desperately that I wrote an anticipation of it in a play: I imagined a woman, Paulina, who believes she recognizes the doctor who raped and tortured her during a dictatorship all too similar to the one in Chile and, aware that the newly elected democratic government of her country cannot try him, decides, when her enemy walks into her beach house, to tie him to a chair and act as both judge and executioner. I let Paulina loose on that doctor, let her say to him the things I would have said, so many of us would have shouted from the rooftops in Chile if we had not suffocated our desires, if we had not been afraid that to speak out would destabilize our transition, if we had not been sure that if we went too far in our demands, the military would come back and punish us yet one more time for daring to rebel.

And yet, even as my imagination ran rampant, even as I savored a society turned upside down and inside out, where the hunted of yesterday became the hunters of today, even in a play where the author supposedly can write whatever he wants, I found myself reluctantly prodding Paulina toward an ending she did not want and I did not want and yet was there, waiting for her and the people of Chile: My protagonist, having tried to bring some personal measure of justice to the world, sits down, when all is said and done, in a concert hall in close and uncanny proximity to the doctor she thinks damaged her irreparably, both of them sharing the same space, the same music, the same peaceful and miserable and lying land. In *Death and the Maiden*, I could not, Paulina could not, fantasize another ending. The tragedy of my country and of so many other precarious democracies worldwide was that we could not put the murderers and violators on trial. That was the pact we signed, the consensus we reached. We thought—and we were probably right—that our ambiguous freedom depended on coexisting with the dictator's shadow and with more than his shadow. Coexisting with his threats, with his oblivion of our memories, with his command that people like Paulina be silenced and ignored and excluded. With his presence as senator for life in a Senate that he himself closed down when he took power in 1973.

Is that the truth of who we are? The sad fact that the resistance was not strong enough to overthrow Pinochet and the glorious fact that we were able, nevertheless, to make the country ungovernable and to negotiate him out of office? The truth we have to swallow because we cannot deny it: The large minority of the country that adores Pinochet and controls the armed forces and most of the economic power will react violently if he is touched.

In the play, that brutal truth was proclaimed by Paulina's husband, Gerardo, a human rights lawyer who defends the doctor who may have raped his wife and pleads with her for that life. A decent and flawed man who wants to save his land more suffering.

And now, suddenly, that truth has exploded. Suddenly, what we could not do, what we desired and also feared, has come to pass, foreign forces have accomplished what Paulina dared only to attempt in the privacy of her home. Will that land also explode?

It is what I ponder as I travel home, back to Chile for the first time since General Pinochet has been arrested less than a month ago. I am returning to host, with my friend Antonio Skármeta (of *Il Postino* fame), a group of South African and Australian writers who are coming to

Chile to find out what joins our Southern countries, discover far from the North the deep and subtle ties that bind us to one another. When we made the original plans for the "Writing the Deep South Conference" more than a year ago, we had not an inkling that Pinochet would be in London under house arrest and the country in turmoil. We are going to have to show Nadine Gordimer and Peter Carey, André Brink and Helen Garner, Zakes Mda and Wally Serote, a land which is heading in a direction that we ourselves are not sure of.

What will we find?

Are we ready to listen to our many Paulinas? Can we break away from the addictive relationship we have formed with a dictator who has been acting like an abusive parent all these years, locking his children in and not letting them speak their minds? And if we begin to speak out, will we be inviting the forces that tore Chile apart in the not-so-distant past to once again confront each other with increased ferocity and destroy the transition?

Every time I have asked myself these questions in the past, Pinochet was always there to answer them, in the dark, toxic center of everything, the outer restricting boundary of what we could and could not do.

Now he has been taken away and we are alone with ourselves.

Will it be different this time?

• • • • •

Ariel Dorfman

I have been trying to draw close to Pinochet, to close in on him. But there is a danger in that closeness. It may, in fact, even be lethal to get too near to him.

Take the case of José Tohá.

I had always admired Tohá, one of Chile's finest journalists, and was pleased to find out, when I started dating my wife, Angélica, back in the 1960s, that he had been like an uncle to her, a bosom friend of her father. She told me that José had held her on his knees and told her stories. I could picture the scene: Angélica is petite and, as a child, was certainly even smaller, and José Tohá was extremely tall, not only by Chilean standards, and very thin and, with his goatee and his slow and deliberate courtesy, oddly resembled Don Quixote. Those were not, of course, the only memories she had of him: Mainly she remembered him spending long hours with her own journalist father, drinking coffee interminably, discussing politics, working for a free Chilean press and dreaming of a liberated Chile.

Tohá got to serve that vision of a different sort of country when in 1970 Salvador Allende named him as his Ministro del Interior, the most important post in the cabinet, the man who becomes vice president when the president travels abroad. Later on, for several years, Tohá took on the delicate role of Minister of Defence. That is how he got to know General Pinochet and his wife, Lucía, how Tohá and his wife, Moy, came to believe that Augusto and Lucía were their friends. On July 10, 1973, in fact, only three months before the coup, when Tohá had ceased to be Minister of Defense, Pinochet had sent a personal note to him saying that he hoped they would get together when Lucía came back from a trip, assuring José and Moy of their enduring friendship.

It was in the name of that friendship, of the presents Pinochet had given to the Tohá children in the past (tin soldiers for their little boy!), of the evenings they had shared, that Moy went to see the General at his offices in the Edificio Diego Portales one day in mid-March of 1974. Perhaps trusting in that friendship, José Tohá had voluntarily surrendered to the insurgents on the day of the coup, six months before, and since then had been sent, along with other former ministers of the Allende government, to Dawson Island, a blustery, cold piece of barren rock off the coast of Patagonia. They were harshly mistreated there, and Tohá more than anyone else—so much so that he had become seriously ill and had been interned in a hospital in nearby Punta Arenas and then flown to a military unit in Santiago. Moy had been informed that her husband was in imminent danger. She had already seen Pinochet a few days after the coup, but in that previous encounter—that will eventually be described later in this book—Moy had been accompanied by two wives of former Ministers, a meeting that, because it was shared with others, had not allowed her to remind Pinochet of the ties of affection that still might bind them. Now, desperate for José, she had decided to ask for a private interview and, surprisingly, after only half a day's delay, had been admitted to Pinochet's presence.

Years later, Moy told me the story of that encounter. I did not take notes and so must rely on the version that she relayed to our mutual friend, perhaps the most astute and persistent journalist in Latin America, Mexican Julio Scherer García:

"He was affable," Moy recollects. "He said to me: 'Madame, what can I do for you?' Treating me with the *Usted* of distance and respect. 'Pardon me,' I answered with the same *Usted*, 'I have not come to speak to the President of the Junta, but with Augusto Pinochet, whom I have known for quite a while.' And then I passed to the more familiar *tú*.

"I said to him: 'I've come to ask you to return my husband to me immediately. I want you to return him to me because he's not well, because there have been problems, because they've now taken him out of the hospital without permission from the doctors. Anything that might happen to him now could be very serious. I need to see him, I need to be with him. I want you to return him to me.'

"He said to me, using the form of *tú* as I had: 'You can't ask that of me. That's not something I can do. Probably the air force has some accusation against your husband. You have to thank me, Moy, that you've asked me for an audience and that this has been agreed to in twelve hours. You've got to think of all the people who have been waiting for months before I receive them.'

"I looked at him strangely. 'You never had to ask for an audience to come to my house. You came when you wanted and you were welcomed. We were friends with both of you, we felt that you were our friends.'

"Pinochet was moving up and down the room. 'I'm not promising anything,' he said. 'Yes, Tohá was cordial with me, and so were you.' But then he started screaming. Saying things like Tencha, Allende's widow, was going to be stripped of her citizenship. He was drinking water and shouting very loudly.

I asked, 'Why are you shouting like that? It's been a long time since I haven't been able to listen to you, even on television, you shout too much.' He answered: 'You're just like my wife. She says that I spend the whole day shouting. But I'm an old man already and I keep on shouting, I can't change.' I said to him: 'Six months ago you were just as old as now, but you were a congenial (*simpático*) old man, now you're just a grumpy (*gruñón*) old man.' Then he looked at me and he smiled. I was reminded a bit of the former General Pinochet whom I had known.

"The minutes went by and I insisted on trying to explain José's situation. 'If I do something,' Pinochet said, 'I'll do it for that little boy who deserves to have a father.' I answered: 'I'll take care of that little boy, that's why I'm his mother. If you do something it will be because you recognize that José is a wonderful human being, the man you got to know so well. If you do something, it is because you respect him.'

"Pinochet kept on pacing around and kept on talking. 'I can't do anything, I can't promise a thing.' As we weren't making any progress, I told him I was leaving. He answered: 'Look, the only thing I can do is hurry the trial up. I'll speak to the prosecutor to make things easier for you, so you can visit your husband.'"

That was the last time Moy saw Pinochet—that old friend who did not keep his promise. Two days later she was informed that José Tohá had hung himself, using his own belt, in the cell he had been locked into at the military hospital.

Moy refuses to believe that version.

José Tohá was in an extreme state of malnutrition, weighing only forty-nine kilos at the moment of his death, and would have been unable to muster the strength to commit suicide. And he was taller than his cell, so it would have been impossible for him to have successfully hung himself in that place.

Conflicting versions. So how can we really know what happened to José Tohá?

Angélica knows. Angélica knew, as soon as I told her, that night in our hotel room, in the exile of that hotel room, that night in March, when I told her that Tohá was dead.

For six months, Angélica had watched the country— and her life—unravel. She had lived through the destruction of her hopes, the dispersal of her family, the murder of her President, she had listened over and over again to stories of friends gone and jailed and killed and banished and she had not shed one tear. Not one tear. Not one. Like so many survivors of extreme trauma she had kept that trauma at bay, she had not let her emotions overwhelm her.

When she heard about Tohá, however, she broke down—she started to cry with a suddenness and brutality that surprised me, that left me bereft, unable to deal with the grief that was shaking her. All she kept on saying, sobbing that one phrase over and over again, was: "*Los van a matar a todos. Los van a matar a todos.*" "They're going to kill all of them, they're going to kill them all."

And yet, a puzzle remains: why José Tohá, one of the most gentle souls I have ever met, precisely the man whom one might have expected a victorious soldier to spare?

Incomprehensible, unless we grasp that this may have been what condemned him to death, that General Pinochet wanted to eliminate anyone who knew that much about him, above all that man who had witnessed him smiling at the ministers of Allende, seen his hands when they had poured wine for their wives, the one man whose mere existence reminded the General of the broken promises of loyalty.

I think that's why José Tohá was murdered.

He had made the mistake of getting too close to General Pinochet.

• • • • •

The Italian news agency ANSA has published a dispatch from its correspondent Mónica Uriel in Madrid, dated

Ariel Dorfman

November 5, 1998, in which details of the questions that Baltasar Garzón has in store for Pinochet have emerged, an inquiry that the Spanish judge is anxious to begin. Having established the list of murdered peasants, workers, students, five executions in Curacaví, thirteen in Osorno, nineteen in Yumbel and Laja, eighteen in Paine, six in Pisagua, twenty-two in Valdivia, four in Cauquenes, thirteen in Mulchén, nine in San Bernardo, seventy-two political prisoners in La Serena, Copiapó, Anotofogasta and Calama, Garzón would then proceed:

How did you give the orders to execute these people? Why did you not apply the Geneva Convention if, as you have declared, you were at war with them and were operating with a battle plan that had public military actions? What sort of hierarchical structure did you use when you gave the orders for those executions to proceed, was it the ordinary military hierarchical structure or was it a paramilitary structure directed by DINA, the secret police? And when did you create DINA? Did this organism depend directly on you, as the head of your secret police, Manuel Contreras, has sworn in a deposition last year? How was a command structure formed that determined which persons were to be kidnapped? And how did DINA coordinate with Argentina, Paraguay and Uruguay, and specifically with Argentine admiral Eduardo Massera, actions such as Operation Colombo—where the bodies of 119 Chileans who had disappeared in Chile were unearthed in Argentine territory and given Argentine identities? And regarding

Operation Condor, and the attempt in Rome to murder the former Chilean Vice President Bernardo Leighton by the neofascist Italians Licio Gelli and Stefano delle Chiaie, what did you say to them when you met them in Madrid where you had gone for the funeral of Franco in 1975? Were those relationships coordinated directly from Chile or through the Chilean Embassy in Rome?

And there are other questions about the assassination in Buenos Aires in October 1974 of the former Commander in Chief of the Army, General Carlos Prats. Why did the Chilean Consulate deny him and his wife a passport when he insisted that he wished to leave Argentina because he felt endangered? And how do you respond to the confession by the same paramilitary commando who carried out the murder of Orlando Letelier in Washington and the attempted murders in Rome and Mexico, how do you respond to the confession by these same agents that they were also responsible for the car bomb that killed General Prats and his wife?

And Pinochet, according to those who have seen the questions that Garzón is preparing, would then be handed a list of 510 Chilean officers, starting with the said Manuel Contreras, so that the man who was once Commander in Chief of the Army and had personally approved the promotion of each of those officers, could identify them one by one and state which operations they were charged with and how they received orders.

And some other questions I have been wanting to ask as well and that are not included in Garzón's list:

Ariel Dorfman

Tell me, General, what you were doing on September 12, 1973, at the Tacna Regiment? Do you remember a wall made from the barrels of discarded rifles, a railing through which you could see what was happening in the next room, see without being seen? Do you remember watching the collaborators of President Allende tortured in that room on the other side of that railing? Claudio Jimeno and Enrique París and Jorge Klein and Jorge Barros and Arsenio Poupin, the men who had seen you interact with Allende day after day? How do you respond to the accusations by retired Major Enrique Cruz, who is at present the head of security of the Chilean Senate, that he saw you there that day, witnessing the torture of those men who only two days before you had smiled at when you met them at La Moneda? Do you deny what retired Major Fernando Reveco has sworn in a deposition, that you were indeed inside that Regiment on that date? And one last question: Did you really need to watch those men being tortured, was that also for the good of the fatherland?

For the good of the fatherland.

Your own words. Used to justify torture.

It was early 1974. Lutheran Bishop Helmuth Frenz and his Catholic counterpart, Bishop Enrique Alvear, had gone to see you in your offices in the Edificio Diego Portales, the enormous building that Salvador Allende had inaugurated three years before when the nations of the world had convened in Santiago for a UN trade conference to discuss how underdeveloped nations could overcome the increasing disparity with the more prosperous countries of the world. Before you overthrew him, Allende had been making plans to turn that mammoth skyscraper into the Palace of the Children of Chile. Now, with La Moneda in ruins, you had made it your palace. That's where you had finally deigned to receive Bishops Frenz and Alvear, the co-presidents of the ecumenical Comité Pro Paz. Do you remember that organization that several of the major religious groups in Chile had founded in order to protect the victims of the dictatorship and that you were very soon to abolish?

Trying not to alienate the president of the Junta already known for his sudden outbursts of rage, the two bishops had decided not to use the word "torture," but "presiones físicas"—physical pressure brought to bear on political prisoners. And yet, it was you yourself who quite unabashedly singled out that uncomfortable word, once you had carefully looked through a thick portfolio of reports that elaborated in agonizing detail what was happening in hundreds of detention centers all over the country. You were the one who interrupted Frenz and Alvear when they tried to explain with circumlocutions what it was that they wanted.

"You mean torture?" you said, when they spoke about presiones físicas.

After Frenz and Alvear assented, you did not interrupt them again until they had finished their litany of complaints, you listened calmly to their demands that such practices come to an end. Then it was your turn to speak:

"Look, you are priests and you work in the Church. You can allow yourself the luxury of being compassionate and benevolent. I'm a soldier and, as head of state, I have a responsibility towards the entire Chilean people. The plague of communism has invaded the people. That's why I need to exterminate communism. The most dangerous Communists are the extremists of the MIR [Movimiento de Izquierda Revolucionario, the Revolutionary Movement of the Left]. They have to be tortured, or they won't sing, if you get my meaning. Torture is necessary to exterminate communism. For the good of the fatherland."

Then you stood up and showed the two bishops to the door. Bishop Helmuth Frenz never saw you again but you did not forget, I am sure, as he never did, that meeting. Did you think to yourself afterward, That was a mistake, I should never have let them know that I know? Or did you simply not care? At any rate, you sent Bishop Frenz one last message, you communicated with him one more time. In June of 1975, when you decided to abolish the Comité Pro Paz, you signed an order expelling the German-born Bishop Frenz. Erasing, you thought, his presence from Chile.

But those words of yours are here, waiting for you in the future that you cannot erase. As you cannot erase the questions that Garzón is about to ask, those questions you will soon have to respond to, one by one, questions that we Chileans have been waiting for more than two decades to ask, that so many of us hope can finally, one by one by one, start to be answered.

•••••

This is the first time in so many years, I murmur to myself, that I will not have to breathe the air he breathes, the first time the General will be away, missing, gone. I repeat it like a mantra, almost a prayer, as if the mere transgressive possibility of thinking it were a way of regressing to a moment in history before I had heard his voice on the other side of the phone, when hardly any of us knew that name, Augusto Pinochet.

Yet there is a puzzling paradox that greets me on this return in mid-November of 1998. Never has General Pinochet been more omnipresent in this country than now when he is in London under temporary arrest, still at the very core and crux of our existence, even more current and crucial now that he is physically absent. This is a country obsessed with General Pinochet. His picture hounds me from a thousand windows full of patriotic flags that demand his release, his eyes scrutinize me from the newspapers ("The Most Important Chilean of the Century," a right-wing rag proclaims in a special supplement about his life), his name is smeared on every wall ("Pinocchio—your crimes have no frontiers"), his case is on every lip, each person I meet discusses his future as if it were ours, as if there were no other theme in the universe. The remote and old and sick General is entangled in our dreams and desires as never before, floating in our minds, dividing us in ways that had seemed to have been overcome since the right and the left decided to coexist

Ariel Dorfman

so democracy could return to Chile. Part of the country is indignant at what is called an affront to national pride and independence; a larger part sees Pinochet's arrest as a final reckoning, long overdue, a form of divine justice; and many in between feel uncomfortable and ambiguous, their hearts saying they want him on trial while their reason suggests that democracy might be undermined, anxious that such a critical issue in our destiny is being decided elsewhere, in Madrid and London. I had felt a similar sense of disquiet during my daily ceremonies as I listened to the BBC news bulletins in the dark before dawn. There is something basically unsound and sick about a country whose ultimate fate depends on Spanish judges, English police forces, a British home secretary who may or may not be true to the utopian ideals of his youth. Victims rather than protagonists, we run the risk of ending up forever alone with Pinochet's malignant shadow, unable to purge his legacy, unable to confront him in our own land and our own language.

People here are trying to get on with life, but it is not easy. Just the other day, as I took some time off from our Australian and South African writer friends and strolled with my wife through the center of the city, we heard loud drums beating, saw faraway red banners waving in the warm spring breeze, guessed it was some sort of march to demand the General's extradition from England to Spain. Not so: A motley crew of around one hundred students, dressed like medieval buffoons, their faces painted all sorts of colors, several of them on gigantic stilts, were parading through one of Santiago's main streets inviting the public to a Festival of University Theater, a sort of Edinburgh Fringe here in our nation's capital. I loved how they jumped, they juggled, they played the fools, dancing their joy at being alive, taking over the rather staid Chilean public space with their carnivalesque celebration of art.

When they had passed, however, not twenty yards behind them another sort of group appeared, marching slowly and solemnly over that very same cement: the mothers and daughters and wives of the disappeared, the association of relatives of prisoners who had been executed without a trial, the movement against torture. These were the women whom I had witnessed for the last twenty or so years, day after day, keeping the flame of memory burning, unwilling to forget their murdered, damaged loved ones, what had been done to those loved ones in some slippery, unspeakable cellar in this same city. They have waited for the day when the man who has mocked them, insulted them, arrested them, beaten them, refused to apologize for what he did, when that man would have to answer for his deeds. They have waited for this day when they would be free to accuse him and he would not be free to ignore their existence. They were singing quietly down the street, hands locked, photos of their dead pinned to their dresses, reminding me and the other bystanders who were out shopping or licking an ice-cream cone or about to take in a movie that there was an abyss between the rollicking, multicolored university students who had just careened through these very streets, drumming and whistling, and the unbearable pain of these women who would not forget, a chasm of memory that needs to be traveled and bridged. Chile is a country where something as normal and wondrous as the young delighting in their own energy and merriment is being challenged by a traumatic past that refuses to be buried. A country where we cannot get on with life until the life that was destroyed right here has been acknowledged.

The distance between these two Chiles, how far we have to journey collectively before the day when we can be an independent and unbroken land, was accentuated and complicated almost immediately by the presence of a third Chile. A middle-aged woman pushed by me as I watched the Mothers of the Disappeared march grimly by, and muttered under her breath, but loud enough for many to hear: "Communist garbage! Liars! *Mentirosos.* We should have killed the lot of them."

Here was a supporter of General Pinochet, someone who no doubt saw in him a savior of the fatherland, fuming at the idea that the man who had created the foundation for a free-market Chile should be in jail. She is part of an extremely vocal, indeed vociferous, right-wing minority who have taken to the streets in feverish numbers. Listening to her spit out those words, the rigid fury in her body, her recalcitrant inability to understand what those victims of the dictatorship had been through, I was taken back to the worst moments of the fascist protests against the democratic government of Salvador Allende in the early seventies. I felt a knot of fear coil inside my stomach. I had seen what that anger could do, where it could lead. I was remembering the long years of Pinochet's rule, when people like this belligerent woman had all the power and believed they could do whatever they wanted and never be held accountable. The General was and still remains the anchor of their identity.

There are many like her in Chile and they continue to wield an extraordinary influence. They have threatened to paralyze the country unless Pinochet is returned safe and sound; they have sent death threats to artists and politicians warning them that if their hero dies abroad, blood will run; they have chanted abuse (and thrown garbage) at the British and Spanish embassies for hours, proclaiming themselves the defenders of the nation against foreign aggression, and, yes, ridiculous as this may sound, colonialism. Their enclaves in business, in the armed forces, in Parliament, pressure the present government of Chile to do more, to recall the ambassadors, to defend not only Pinochet's diplomatic immunity but his innocence as well. Or else.

These are the turbulent waters that the democratic, center-left government of President Eduardo Frei must navigate and so we contemplate the absurd spectacle of men who were persecuted and exiled by Pinochet, who in their deepest heart would like nothing more than to see him chastened and put on trial here in Chile, we see these officials—among them, a couple of my best friends!—trapped into arguing his cause and the need for

Chile to take care of its own affairs; we see these men trying to keep alive a consensus that has made the nation governable, trying to preserve the unity of a country that is being pulled apart at the seams. They point to a series of investigations that Chilean Judge Juan Guzmán is slowly but tenaciously carrying out, in which Pinochet has been accused of torture and disappearance, an inquiry that has not yet led to any indictments and which, quite frankly, I do not believe (along with most people in Chile) can possibly lead anywhere. The army would never let its beloved leader be humiliated in a Chilean court. In the best of cases, it would insist that he be tried in front of a military court that would then declare him innocent. And as Senator for Life he has parliamentary immunity.

Given the complex situation I have just described, it is not strange that many prominent Chileans (and not only right-wing accomplices of the dictatorship's crimes) proclaim that the British High Court, in its recent ruling that Pinochet must be sent back, is in fact helping Chile to continue with a transition that so far has gone smoothly. It is time, they say, to stop the Spanish Judge Garzón and the English government from meddling in our history, troubling our peace.

I disagree. Detention in a foreign land reminds us of the deepest truth about our recent history, slaps us into understanding the truth we have been hiding from: that we have been, we still are, hostages of General Pinochet.

The time has come to change this situation, this sham reconciliation that demanded that one victimized group of citizens forget the suffering visited upon them without demanding that the dominant group of privileged and ignoble citizens who had inflicted that suffering on their fellow Chileans ever seek forgiveness. This national crisis reveals just how fragile and insecure our transition really was. If our foreign friends have intervened in our internal affairs, it is because we have not intervened in them ourselves. If they can remind us so shockingly of the terror of the victims, it is because we have not, as a nation, remembered that terror sufficiently. If they believe it is legitimate to judge Pinochet, it is because we have not dared to judge him. And though we obviously need a trial with Chilean judges, I believe a more elementary and fundamental sort of probing of our own humanity must preface and prepare and accompany that possible public reckoning. As a community, we have to confront our past, strip that past naked even if it leaves us trembling and troubled. We have to look each other in the eye and tell each other the truths we have hidden, the joy we felt at the pain of our fellow countrymen. We have to exhibit our fears, take the distress of our bruised victims into our lives, assign responsibilities for the tragedy we have lived, demand that those who killed the innocent be banished from public office and the armed forces and, what may be, at least for me, the most difficult duty of all, recognize how profoundly General Pinochet is part of our history, representing something deep and terrible in our identity. This is what the foreign nations who are suddenly so central to my nation's life are telling us:

Ariel Dorfman

Chile must find the moral strength, once and for all, to truly complete its transition to democracy.

That is the urgent task, far too often postponed, the task we need to undertake if we want a different sort of country, where young students prancing their love of life through downtown Santiago will never again find themselves followed by the footsteps of sorrow of the relatives of the Disappeared and the Dead. The task of extracting Pinochet from our minds, turning him into a terrible memory that will not return.

A task nobody can do in our stead, a task that neither the English nor the Spanish can save us from. A task that awaits us whether the General remains abroad or whether they send him back to this Santiago where he continues to be dismally present, almost as if he had never left.

●●●●●

Does it mean anything that the House of Lords has been convened to hear the decision of the five Law Lords on precisely November 25, 1998, precisely for Pinochet's eighty-third birthday? Is it because the Judges wish to give him his freedom as a present? Or are they playing a cruel joke on him and have chosen his birthday because they will overturn the ruling by the High Court that would deny his extradition to Spain?

There is expectation in the august chamber of Westminster. Each of the Law Lords will rise and speak in turn, each one quite briefly, referring colleagues, lawyers, onlookers and journalists to the extensive written briefs that justify their opinions.

First to rise is Lord Slynn of Hadley. "My Lords," he says, "for the reasons set out in the speech which I have prepared and which is available in print, I would hold that the respondent, as a former head of state, is immune from arrest in the matters alleged in the warrant of October 22, 1998, and I would dismiss the appeal."

One for Pinochet. Zero for Garzón.

But really: One for the idea that heads of state cannot be judged by courts of other nations; zero for the movement that would establish universality of jurisdiction for crimes against humanity, an aspiration which, according to Lord Slynn, is merely embryonic at this stage and which does not have a widely supported consensus.

Next to speak is Lord Lloyd of Berwick: "In my opinion, the State of Chile is entitled to claim immunity on behalf of Senator Pinochet under the terms of the State of Immunity Act of 1978 and at common law. I would therefore dismiss the appeal."

Two for Pinochet. Zero for Garzón.

Lord Lloyd argues in his written opinion that if Pinochet is to be judged, he could only be judged in a court in his own land or by an international tribunal expressly created for that purpose, but not by a foreign court, unless Chile had waived state immunity (which of course, Chile has not). So it is zero votes for judging him internationally and two votes for national sovereignty.

Will Pinochet be heading back to Chile today?

Lord Nicholls of Birkenhead stands up: "For the reasons set out in a speech which I have prepared in draft, I would reverse the decision of the Divisional Court, allow this appeal and hold that the respondent Senator Pinochet is not immune from the criminal process of this country, of which extradition forms part."

Two for Pinochet. One for Garzón.

In the core of his written comments, Lord Nicholls explains that "international law has made plain that certain types of conduct, including torture and hostage-taking, are not acceptable conduct on the part of anyone. This applies as much to heads of state, or even more so, as it does to everyone else; the contrary conclusion would make a mockery of international law." Since the end of the Second World War and the Nuremberg trials, he states, "no head of state could have been in any doubt about his potential personal liability if he participated in acts regarded by international law as crimes against humanity."

Now it is Lord Steyn's turn: "For the reasons contained in my speech, copies of which are available to the parties, I would allow the appeal. The effect of my speech is that, in a correct interpretation of the law, General Pinochet has no immunity whatsoever."

It's a draw, two against two.

Lord Steyn, originally a South African who has been

said to have opposed apartheid, is particularly worried about the possibility that, under the arguments presented by Pinochet's defense, Hitler himself would have been absolved, as he would have been acting as a head of state when he committed his crimes: "The development of international law since the Second World War justifies the conclusion that by the time of the 1973 coup d'état, and certainly ever since, international law condemned genocide, torture, hostage taking and crimes against humanity (during an armed conflict or in peace time) as international crimes deserving of punishment."

All eyes turn to Lord Leonard Hoffmann, also born in South Africa. He pauses before speaking, takes his time, knowing that his is the decisive vote. "I have the advantage of reading the draft of the speeches of my noble learned friends, Lord Nicholls of Birkenhead and Lord Steyn. I agree with them that Senator Pinochet does not have immunity from prosecution and I too therefore would allow the appeal."

Eyewitnesses say that gasps went up from the chamber and that Lord Hoffmann glanced in the direction of the people in the galleries who had echoed the gasps with a sort of hushed cheer of their own. As if Lord Hoffmann understood that the real importance of his tie-breaking decision was how it affected not the Law Lords themselves, but the general public, how the ruling that Pinochet had no immunity and could stand trial would influence human rights and international law for decades to come.

Ariel Dorfman

Nobody comments that, of the five Law Lords, Lord Hoffmann is the only one who has not justified his concurrence with a written opinion of any kind.

Except Pinochet's lawyers. As will be clear in the months to come, they have noted Lord Hoffmann's reticence.

The trial of Pinochet has hardly begun.

• • • • •

As for me, I am afraid.

First comes the joy, it is true, when I hear—again glued to the radio, again back here in my home in North Carolina this November 25, 1998—that the Law Lords have ordered the extradition of Pinochet to proceed. And yet, I must recognize, even as I celebrate this victory against impunity, just underneath the exultation something else emerges. Yes, it is fear that I am feeling.

I do not like this fear that so suddenly assaults me, that does not allow me to innocently enjoy this defeat of dictators from all over the globe. Even so, I clutch onto this dread because it helps me to better understand the country I unfortunately share with Pinochet, it connects me with the state of mind of all my compatriots, whether they are adversaries or supporters of the General.

In my recent trip back home, that fear may have been the one consistent underlying emotion inside every man and woman who crossed my path—and because I was acting as a guide to foreign authors, the lot of us managed and indeed needed to meet hundreds of Chileans from all stations of life. Over and over, a shrugging of the shoulders, a turning away, a casting down of the eyes before they darted up: proof of a trauma that has not been overcome in eight years of democracy. Proof that the coup is still happening somewhere behind the eyes, unraveling like a newsreel that we cannot turn off. "It's that you don't know how it was..." and "We've suffered so much..." and "My sister-in-law was raped, they jailed my best friend for seven months and he lost his job, still doesn't have it back, they returned Dad to us all broken, as if he were a torn rag" and "You just can't understand what it meant, those years." Over and over again, the same words from different mouths. Repeating the same festering suspicion, inflamed by an orchestrated campaign of terror from Pinochet's followers, that those dark times of censorship and death can return.

When Antonio Skármeta and I took our guests to the tiny seaside hamlet of Isla Negra to visit the house of Pablo Neruda, our greatest poet—who died, as much of cancer as of heartbreak, a few days after the September 11 coup—we had an intriguing conversation with some schoolchildren somewhere between the ages of eight and ten, who, to our astonishment, did not know what the word *dictatorship* meant. "Hey, that's not possible. How can you kids not know that word?" we asked. "No, no, we don't know what it means," they said. And their teacher, after many twists and cautious turns in the exchange, after she had felt that we could be trusted and

Ariel Dorfman

after she had told us how bad things had been ("It's that you simply can't understand what it was like..."), confessed that if she were to inform her charges about that word, their parents—most of them opponents of Pinochet—would have scratched the offending syllables from the notebook, would have protested against their boys and girls being indoctrinated with politics at school. The consequences and remnants and dregs of that dictatorship which the children cannot name, which their parents do not wish to name, continue to poison the Chile of the transition.

And I do understand that fear because it is the one that overwhelms me now in North Carolina, the fear that engorged me a week ago in Santiago when, one night, I received an urgent phone call from someone with *very good contacts* who informed me that the army was quartered in its barracks, a state of emergency was about to be declared, that General Ricardo Izurieta, Pinochet's successor as Commander in Chief who up till now had quelled dissent within the ranks, had lost control of the situation and that a coup was imminent. A contraction of panic contorted my stomach, screamed at me silently to be careful, that I had to find a place to hide my Australian and South African friends, that they should call their embassies just in case...because anything was possible, everything was possible. Remember that Colonel Pedro Ewing, the Army spokesperson, had warned the public that the armed forces were taking careful note of how each person had acted in the Pinochet case. They had ingrained deep in their minds, Ewing said, the names of those who had been against Pinochet.

It was an irrational panic attack that rapidly dissolved as soon as I was able to command a cold analytic approach to the facts. A military uprising was unthinkable, there were no conditions for such an adventure. I myself had written as much in the preceding months, answering the fear-mongers who want to scare us into getting Pinochet back: Democracy was not in danger. And I am able to perform, one week later, the same sobering dissection of the truth now that General Pinochet will have to appear in front of a tribunal to hear for the first time the charges against him, to plead innocent or guilty: The country is stable and mature enough to face that test.

But if I cannot avoid that apprehension—I who live safely abroad, I who am protected by my writing and my media and political connections—how will my fellow countrymen react, what hidden uncertainties will churn just below their surface calm, their smile of satisfaction at the news that Pinochet is to be dragged into court?

Of course that fear I felt and the fear of the many Chileans who were the prey of Pinochet is not the only sort that persists in my country. There is another fear, of a different, more dangerous kind, far more difficult to quench...

The last day of this recent visit of mine to Santiago I took a taxi up to the barrio of La Reina to see my mother-in-law. It was driven by an elderly woman, rather on the skinny side, who was attentively listening to a local call-in show on the radio. One of the guests on the show, Carmen Hertz, had just resigned her post as the director of the Ministry of Foreign Affairs International Juridical Division because she had to become a party in a case brought in front of Chilean Judge Juan Guzmán who was investigating the disappearance of Carmen's husband, Carlos Berger, who had been executed in 1973 in Calama in a rampage of killings by a military expedition organized by Pinochet. During fifteen minutes, the woman who was driving the taxi and myself, her only passenger, heard Carmen Hertz explain, speaking for all the other widows of the country, how Chile would have no real reconciliation until the man who was ultimately responsible for their sorrow was judged.

And then a listener called in. She said that all of this mess was not the fault of Pinochet but of that criminal Allende. Allende was the one who had started the terror; Pinochet had been forced to save the country from communism, from the thousands of Cuban terrorists who had infiltrated the land. She claimed that her father's property, a large hacienda, had been expropriated by the allendistas and that was a violation of her family's human rights that nobody wanted to remember.

Carmen Hertz and the journalist who was interviewing her reminded the woman who had called in that there had never been any proof of the thousands of Cuban terrorists and went on to analyze the difference between threatening a piece of property and somebody's body, the difference between expropriating a farm and putting rats up someone's anus and then making him disappear without a trace. Agreeing with them, I nevertheless was aware that these distinctions would be irrelevant to the caller. She had lived as a trauma Allende's attempt to dispossess her of the family estate, she had lived it as an assault upon her most intimate identity, and anything done to the barbarians who had persecuted her was fully justified. She felt herself to be the victim, rescued by Pinochet, who acted as a *Tata*, the patriarch who was the guarantor of her right to exist. How to reach her, that woman who had celebrated each one of our sufferings during those seventeen years? That woman who had opened a bottle of champagne upon hearing of Allende's death? That woman corroded by a fear which, subjective and petty as it might be, was not for her less true than ours with our multiple exiles and corpses and pain? How to enter into a dialogue with her and with that gigantic third of the Chilean population who, like her, conjured us up as the enemy that would, given the chance, once again steal her property, enslave and kill her, rape her daughters? How to overcome the blind hatred of that woman, her inability to feel the afflictions of others as if they were her own? How to make her listen to us now that her hero was jailed and she felt that her world and certainties were crumbling, if she is firmly convinced that only a return of authoritarianism and military rule will make us understand that they won this war and we lost it?

That is the minute, meticulous story of Chile in our times: Though I have never even met that woman, she is afraid of me and I am terrified of her.

Ariel Dorfman

And I do not know how to resolve the abyss that separates us. With Pinochet under arrest or with Pinochet free, I do not know how to share a country with her.

But that is not how this story ends.

Before descending from the taxi, that day in Santiago, I asked the lady driver what she does if a passenger complains about the sort of program she was listening to, one of the few of its sort in Chile that allows Pinochet's victims to bear witness to their distress and desires.

She looked at me in the rearview mirror.

"If they don't like the program," she told me, "then I'll lower the volume. But I keep listening."

"And if they ask you to switch it off?"

The lady turned to look me straight in the eyes. No rearview mirror.

"I don't care what they ask me."

"And you've never had to switch off a program that you wanted to listen to? Because you were, say, afraid?"

"Never," she answered. "I'm in my taxi. If they don't like it, they can get out. Why should I be afraid?"

She's the one I think of now, one week later. I let the memory of that small, almost emaciated woman flood back to me, ridding me of my possible terror, helping me to relish the moment when Pinochet, on the other side of the planet, was informed that he would not be able to escape his past and our past.

That's what I hold on to: the calm, quiet look of that old woman who drove a taxi in Santiago as she parked her car so I could get out, her hand which did not tremble as she raised the volume of the radio so that she and all her passengers could keep on hearing the story of Chile which far too many of our compatriots do not yet want to admit, the story of grief and resistance that we all need to hear if we are to be truly free, if we hope to conquer our fear.

•••••

Yesterday, December 11, 1998, for the first time in his life, General Pinochet finally had to face a court of law. His lawyers had done everything they could to avoid the arraignment by the presiding magistrate Graham Parkinson in the case of *The King of Spain versus Augusto Pinochet Ugarte.* They had tried to get Jack Straw, the British home secretary, to dismiss the case. Straw refused to do so, authorizing the extradition to proceed. There were no humanitarian reasons to invoke, though they could be brought up again in the future. The fact that Straw had chosen December 10, Human Rights Day (the day in 1948 when the United Nations adopted its Universal Declaration of Human Rights), sent the additional, barely unspoken message to the General that relief was not in sight from the British government. And as Pinochet's lawyers had already petitioned the Court to excuse the former dictator, due to his frail health, from appearing in person, and the magistrate had answered that the defendant seemed in good enough condition to make the short trip to the court adjoined to Belmarsh

Ariel Dorfman

prison in South London from his refuge in Surrey, the General could not finally avoid being wheeled into the courthouse.

It was not yet my old and persistent dream come true: The only question he had to answer was his name ("My name is Augusto Pinochet Ugarte," he answered in Spanish. "I was Commander in Chief of the Army in Chile, Captain-General of Chile, President of the Republic, and at the moment Senator of the Republic") and no victims looked him in the eye and nobody answered his claims that all the charges were "lies of those men from Spain." And no cameras captured his hands, naked and ungloved according to witnesses, clutching a walking stick.

But something very drastic happened in that Belmarsh courthouse. Not something merely symbolic. For some people at least, the world had suddenly been turned upside down. For some people, life would never be the same.

One of those is a Chilean handyman I will call Rolando. Maestro Rolando has been doing odd jobs for us in Chile, on and off for the last ten years: carpentry, painting, plumbing, a bit of everything. Someone who can fix any problem we have in the house we keep there—and do it with a great dry sense of humor to boot. He's had dozens of conversations with my wife, Angélica—but today she called me from Santiago to tell me that yesterday, when the Maestro had sat down to lunch after a morning dedicated to fixing leaks and a door that kept jamming, he had, for the first time since they had met, revealed to her the most direful experience in his life.

A few years after the coup—Angélica said he spoke in a matter-of-fact voice—he had been arrested and tortured by General Pinochet's police. Rolando worked back then as a porter in a school and his tormentors wanted him to implicate his colleagues, finger any teachers who might be engaged in subversive activities. It had been a brief detention. Two, three, days, and then they'd let him go. He'd lost his job, suffered bodily pain for a few months, and psychological damage for who knows how long. And had kept silent. Till now.

Now he was able, suddenly, to speak about what had happened to him. For more than twenty years, like millions of other Chileans, he had shut himself inside the closet of his secret emotions, had only murmured the tale to his own inner shadow. Strangely enough, it was not Pinochet's arrest on October 16, 1998, that had freed Rolando's voice, but the decision by Britain's highest court to confirm that arrest and then the General's humiliation in that courthouse in Belmarsh. That had done it: the faraway British lords whispering to Maestro Rolando that Pinochet was not above or beyond the law, the subsequent journey the former dictator had been forced to make to face an indictment, the six English policemen who escorted him into that room, the fact that Pinochet's lawyer had asked Magistrate Parkinson to grant his client permission to walk in the garden. There it was, the proof of the General's vulnerability and decline. If he wanted to walk in the garden, he had to ask permission!

It was, our handyman said, as if an enormous burden had been lifted from his body, as if he was being granted permission to finally let his hidden words flow into the vast public space of Chile. Because Maestro Rolando was now free in his own country and the man responsible for ravaging that country was under arrest in a foreign land.

Angélica added that Maestro Rolando was also happy for another reason: He had bet the local owner of a *botillería* that Pinochet would lose the case in England and last night he had claimed his two bottles, one of good red wine and another of *pisco,* our special Chilean brandy. He had drunk them with friends. Nor was he alone in his celebration. In *poblaciones* all over Chile, men and women, Angélica informed me, had poured spontaneously into the streets, beating drums, chanting, dancing—the sort of collective joy that my country had not witnessed since democracy returned eight years ago. An explosion in the streets that echoed the surfacing of Rolando's story: people taking back their right to express themselves. People ceasing to hide. People recognizing each other as soul mates in their search for a new land.

No matter what happens in the future, no one can take this away from us: A man finds his voice after so many decades of silence and shame.

A man who is pouring himself a glass of wine under the Chilean mountains.

While Pinochet takes a solitary walk in his frigid British garden.

•••••

General Pinochet does not only believe in God. He also believes that God believes in him. Saving him over and over again for his divine and messianic mission.

He told journalist Mónica González in September of 1995: "There was no dictatorship in Chile. We are an example for the whole world. The fall of the Berlin Wall was caused by Chile, we were the first to raise our flags against the Berlin Wall, we were the first to defeat Communism." And he added: "I wish to be remembered as the best president Chile ever had."

•••••

It was a day in October of 1951 that I first heard of the Abraham Lincoln Brigade. A nine-year-old child on his first visit to Europe, I was standing on the frontier that separates France from Spain. My Argentine father—a former Communist and still very much a man of the left— had sworn, like so many of his generation who had *España en el corazón*, that he would never step on Spanish soil until Franco was gone or dead. But we swear many things in life, and life makes demands of us that are not always heroic or definitive; life has a way of confronting us with what Primo Levi called the gray zones.

My father was working at the time at the United Nations in New York, and he had professional business to conduct in Madrid and Barcelona. And so we came to the frontier of the country he had vowed he would never visit in his lifetime, even though it had been his emotional center ever since its struggle against fascism in the thirties had inspired him and countless millions around the world. We had been traveling from France and, because the tracks were narrow-gauge on the Spanish side, it was necessary to descend in Irún and change trains. My father took me by the hand and walked me to the very edge of Spanish territory. He crouched down to my height so he could look me in the eyes and told me that this was the place where the Republic had been betrayed.

Here, he said, right here, the weapons that the Republic had paid for had been blocked by the French, with the acquiescence of the English and the Americans. Proclaiming their neutrality, these countries, future allies against Germany, had conspired to starve the Republic, not realizing that they were, in fact, encouraging and appeasing Hitler and Mussolini. Did I know who Hitler and Mussolini were?

I nodded my head solemnly.

Hitler's aircraft, my father said, and Mussolini's ground troops were engaged on the side of Franco. And I knew who Franco was because he was the *hijo de puta* who governed this land and whose name I shouldn't mention while we were in Spain. Even then, as a child, I was being trained, as my own children would be many years later in Chile, to hide my thoughts from the men in power, to hide what our family really thought about Franco.

Franco—my father twisted the word in his mouth as if it hurt him merely to say it. Here is where the Second World War began, my father said. Never forget that here is where the Spanish were betrayed.

My father was crying as he said this, his hand trembling in my hand. I can't remember having seen him cry before that. My father, who is well over ninety years of age now, was and still is a man of steel, not one to vent his emotions. And I can only recall him ever crying again, once, when he told me, at another train station, in Buenos Aires some years later, that his own father had died.

Those tears of his, falling slowly on the Spanish frontier, certainly had the effect that he desired: I have never forgotten what Spain meant to him, how the loss of the Spanish Civil War was one of the great tragedies of his life and, I was later to learn, one of the great tragedies of a century that has seen its fill.

The antidote to the tears came soon. As soon as the train began chugging south to Madrid, my father told me another story, in hushed, low tones: the story of the International Brigades, and particularly of the Lincoln Brigade. Or maybe he used the word *battalion.* How its members had poured into this country to counteract the spread of the black shirts, the decisive battles they had won, *el Ejército del Ebro* that had crossed the river and beaten the Falangistas.

Ariel Dorfman

For me, in 1951, the existence of the Lincoln Brigade did not work merely as a legendary story of heroism, of men and women willing to give their lives for the cause of democracy while their governments stood by and watched the Republic bleed to death. Though born in Buenos Aires, I was then a Yankee boy who thought of himself as an American. I refused to speak Spanish, sang "The Star-Spangled Banner" with fervor, and professed to anyone who cared to listen (and to many who didn't) that New York was the best city in the best country in the world. Like any little patriot, I was always looking for a reason to justify my love of my adopted home. And yet I was also the son of a father persecuted by McCarthy, a witch-hunt that would eventually lead us to abandon the United States a few years later and head for Chile.

At nine years of age, I was living an irreconcilable contradiction: The country I considered my own was trying to exile my father. The fact that the very United States that was hounding our family and so many of our left-wing *gringo* friends had also produced the Lincoln Brigade was a source of comfort to me and also one of the first profoundly political lessons I received in my life. It confirmed in me something I knew but could barely articulate at the time: There were two Americas, one personified by the FBI and J. Edgar Hoover and Joe McCarthy, the other made up of citizens who were willing to risk their lives for freedom wherever it was threatened, an America that came to be represented more and more in my imagination by the Abraham Lincoln Brigade.

That was the America I could belong to: If these citizens could defy their government in the name of the permanent values that America should really stand for, so could I. If they defined their loyalty to humanity above their loyalty to the short-term interests of the United States, so could I.

The men and women of the Lincoln Brigade could not know that, many years after they had left Madrid, they would rescue a small nine-year-old from confusion and push him toward political maturity. They could not have anticipated that their mere existence would help him to realize that there was another, deeper, and more decent America to which he could pledge allegiance.

Someday I will meet them, I said to myself back then, when those volunteers gave me shelter in a time of need, someday I will be able to thank them.

Strange that it is Pinochet who has allowed this childhood dream—ardently repeated to myself as I grew older—to come true. The veterans of the Lincoln Brigade gather every year in San Francisco to commemorate their past deeds and present struggles and on this occasion, I have been invited to celebrate with them, journeying at the end of February 1999 to the Bay Area, circling back to the place where, four months ago, I had first heard the news of Pinochet's arrest. The surviving combatants have asked me to talk to them about the trial, the chances that the same Madrid which they defended in the battle of Jarama will see Pinochet judged and condemned. As I meet them, first for dinner and then for a lunch next day and yet again

Ariel Dorfman

after my speech and into the night, I find in them a fierce interest in the case that almost rivals that of the relatives of the disappeared and missing. They are old now—mostly men, a few women, all in their eighties and nineties, painfully aware that each passing year sees their ranks dwindle—and they all feel as if they have been handed, at the end of their lives, a wonderful and unexpected offering. For these elderly warriors, who watched Francisco Franco die in his bed without ever having been held accountable for his crimes, there is a special balance being restored to the cosmos by the sweet way that the pendulum of history has swung back, post-Franco Spain judging the ideological heir to Franco, the man who sees himself as carrying on *el Caudillo*'s special mixture of repressively conservative Catholicism with a modernizing capitalist mentality.

But their joy, I discover, goes deeper than their connection to the place where they fought and where Pinochet may someday be punished for his crimes. They see Pinochet's arrest as continuing the same tradition and concept of humanity that they held high when, more than sixty years ago, they volunteered to travel to Spain, defying their own government, and die for a cause in a land where they had not been born, to die next to Germans and French and Russians and Yugoslavs and Latin Americans, defending the right of good men to intervene in the fight against injustice wherever it may exist, defining themselves as human beings first and as members of a nationality second. Anticipating this moment in history when humanity would agree with them that to trample one man's freedom is to trample the freedom of all men. And their ideals have not changed: "We're saving up," one of them tells me, the freckled hand that had carried a rifle in the hills of Catalonia and the fields of Castilla taking in his comrades seated at our long table in a Berkeley restaurant, "in case that trial really happens, to all go over and see your General get his lumps."

And yet, more than crossing the Atlantic to see Pinochet on trial in their Madrid, these veterans envision, as do I, an alternative that is even more satisfying, though it is doubtful if history will accommodate us. These internationalists, who in their day broke down the frontiers created by governments and states, paradoxically remain American, deeply American—and that is, perhaps, what most rankles them: the responsibility of their own country in the creation of Pinochet and the support of his dictatorship. They feel that the United States needs to make amends. By opening its files so that the intervention in Chile to overthrow Allende can be widely known by the public and examined by historians. By standing on the side of Garzón and the victims instead of trying to get the General off the hook. But above all, by demanding his extradition to the United States to answer for the murders of Orlando Letelier and his American assistant Ronni Moffit.

Then the circle would be truly complete.

The day these few veterans of the Lincoln Brigade who are left, the veterans who gave me hope as a child on that frontier in Spain and inspired me as an adolescent and later as a revolutionary in Chile and even later as a wandering bilingual exile for years and years, the day when those veterans can file into a courtroom in Washington, D.C., and watch the self-proclaimed heir to Franco stand there, in front of them, to stand trial as a terrorist, I like to think that that will be the day when the circle that began in the States and wove through Spain and continued on to Chile and back, would be truly compete, truly sweet. In a sense, the Brigadistas would, after so many years, have finally come home.

• • • • •

That you in 1973, being a public official, namely Commander in Chief of the Chilean Army, jointly with others intentionally inflicted severe pain or suffering on Pedro Hugo Arellano Carvajal by:

a) *tying him to a metal bed and forcing his hands against an electrifying metal plate, throwing him across the room from the shock;*

b) *electrocuting him with electric wires attached to his chest, his penis and his toes;*

c) *tying him to a tree and whipping him and driving him down corridors where he was beaten;*

d) *placing him on board a helicopter, pushing him out with ropes tied to his trousers, and dragging him through thorns;*

e) tying him to a rope and lowering him into a well, until he was nearly drowned, pulling him out and lowering him back into the well when he failed to answer questions;

f) subjecting him to "Russian roulette";

g) placing an apple on his head and shooting over his head and having a priest administer last rites to him, asking him to commend his soul to God, collaborating thus with the torturers;

h) forcing him to take his clothes off in the presence of the captive Rodríguez family who had been arrested with their sons, forcing him to witness the torture of that family as the father was forced to lie on top of his sons making him move sexually in such a way that the father penetrated one of the sons and the other son was made to penetrate the smaller one and Pedro Arellano was placed on top of one of the children just like the father and forced to do the same thing. The marines from the infantry who direct these sessions stand above the prisoners putting a bayonet to their neck and tell them that if they do not penetrate the boys they will shoot them through the head. And they then push them naked down corridors continually beating them;

i) opening the anus of one of the children and cutting it with a bayonet;

j) while Pedro Arellano observed how elderly people

were being pelted with stones by the military during half an hour and then were forced to walk on their knees on the runaway full of stones of El Belloto Air Force Base;

and all this was done in purported performance of official duties;

That you jointly with others intentionally inflicted severe pain or suffering on Irma del Carmen Parada González by:

a) by forcing her to listen to the howls of tortured prisoners during two days;

b) stripping her of her clothes;

c) applying electric current to her mouth, vagina and breasts;

d) subjecting her to rape by two men;

e) putting her hands into chemicals and introducing them into a machine, causing her to lose consciousness and when she came to her senses, placing her in a hole with dead bodies and wet straw;

f) forcing her to eat putrid food and the human remains of her dead fellow captives, which she realizes when another prisoner tells her, after she is given her first food in several days, that there is a human ear floating in her soup and that this comes from those already murdered and then she hears a

shot and presumes that the prisoner who warned her
was himself killed by the military;

and all of this in purported performance of official
duties.[2]

One-page excerpt of the indictment by Judge Baltasar
Garzón against General Augusto Pinochet. There are 249
more pages.

• • • • •

**How can it be that Pinochet has managed to fool so many
Chileans? How to explain that so many believed he was
always unaware of the crimes committed under his
regime, still believe him to be innocent today?**

**Yes, his innocence allows his followers to claim the
same sort of ignorance about the horrors that were going
on, yes, his brand of neoliberal free-marketeering made
lots of his countrymen rich and allowed many of the
poorer ones to buy into that dream of prosperity, yes, he
used and abused their fear of Godless socialism, yes, he
appealed to their patriotism and need for strength, order
and authority in confusing times, yes, he controlled all
the media, yes, we can chalk up any number of social and
economic and cultural reasons to explain why he
remains popular among large groups of Chileans—and
not only, by the way, those directly benefiting from his
policies.**

Ariel Dorfman

Take a woman whom I'll call Gracia. One of my wife's dearest pals, a woman who had been the first of Angélica's childhood friends to fully accept me back in the sixties, this foreign-born Jewish intellectual who had come to seduce the local belle, take away the Angélica that everyone had always thought would and should marry a typical *chileno.* I really liked Gracia, immensely enjoyed an almost vulgar vitality that coursed through her, the jolly way in which she faced every adversity life would smack her with. And there were many of them, those adversities. The latest, we discovered when we went to visit her in 1988 at the small rural town where Gracia and Angélica had been brought up, was that she had just lost her job. As a direct result of Pinochet's merciless economic policies, as we were quick to point out over a tea she had prepared for us. Nevertheless, she told us, as she generously offered us all sorts of delicious treats, she was planning to vote for her *Tata* (Grandpa) Pinochet in the upcoming plebiscite, just as she had voted a few years back for his fraudulent constitution.

She listened to my long harangue, my patient political analysis, my detailed diatribe against Chile's leader and the way he was modernizing Chile to enrich a few and not help the many, and when I was done, she just shrugged her shoulders, offered me some more appetizing crushed avocado on toast and said: "I'm going to vote for him anyway."

"But why?" I asked, exasperated. "What about the dead, the executed, the exiled?"

"Oh," Gracia said, "he doesn't know about any of that. Just look at him, our *Tata*, he has such beautiful blue eyes."

How many other Chileans think something similar, have been taken in by something so frivolous and apparently insignificant? Can it be that he has survived, has been able to hide from us, this demon of mine, because of his eyes? Can it be that Pinochet will escape punishment because of his amazingly mild blue eyes?

• • • • •

I happen to be here in London on this twenty-fourth day of March 1999, when the pivotal, determining moment in the Pinochet saga is enacted.

I have flown in from Belfast this morning for an authors luncheon, but I am wrested away from the second course—and that fish dish looked so succulent!—by the need to attend the next phase in the trial. Feeling, I must admit, a faint sense of absurd superiority over my merely literary colleagues who stay behind for the dessert. After all, they don't have *their* own dictator in the dock, his fate about to be announced to the world. And Diane Dixon, of the Victor Jara Foundation, has arranged for Labour Parliamentarians to sneak Angélica and me in to the House of Lords where the verdict regarding Pinochet's extradition is about to be revealed.

What? The House of Lords? Again? Hadn't the Law Lords already determined this matter five months ago?

Well, yes and no.

Remember Lord Hoffmann and his brief, tie-breaking concurrence at the end of last year's November 25 session that overturned the High Court's previous determination that Pinochet, as a former head of state, was immune from prosecution in Spain and England?

A few days after that historic three-to-two ruling, the General's lawyers asked the House of Lords to annul Lord Hoffmann's vote on the grounds that he was biased against the plaintiff, because of his ties to Amnesty International. Lord Hoffmann had not publicly revealed that he was the (unpaid) honorary chairman of that human rights group's independent charitable arm, nor that he represented Amnesty in 1980, nor that his wife, Gillian, had been working in Amnesty's press office since 1977. A different panel of five Law Lords, headed by Lord Browne-Wilkinson, decided to accept the complaint and then ruled, after several days of further hearings, that, rather than cancel Lord Hoffmann's vote, which would have, in effect, left standing the lower Court's decision favorable to Pinochet, they would hold a new set of hearings by seven new Law Lords. This decision to overturn a previous judgment was unprecedented: The only time in all its history that the House of Lords had even deigned to hear a petition for reversal of a pronouncement by their colleagues had been in 1823 and in that case—dealing with property rights—they had declined to set aside the previous ruling. In this instance, however, Lord Browne-Wilkinson and his fellow peers had unanimously considered that the Pinochet case was of such import that there was a supreme need for transparency and impartiality. They were not moved by the arguments of Garzón's lawyers who pointed out that Lord Hoffmann had made rulings in the past in favor of upholding the death penalty, even if that went against Amnesty's charter, or that the attorneys defending Pinochet had themselves contributed to Amnesty in the past, or that those same attorneys had always known of Lord Hoffmann's connections to that human rights organization and had not raised any original objection to his presence on the panel (in order, rumors suggest, to be able to assail his judgment if it went against them).

Which is why, on this day in late March, I find myself squeezed into a seat in the upper gallery of the House of Lords. Barely able to fit into this cramped space spilling over with spectators, many of them "baddies," according to the Labour member of Parliament who has smuggled us in, conservative backbenchers who think that their hero Pinochet will be freed today. Their presence and cheerfulness adds to my apprehension. Several of the Law Lords who invalidated the earlier ruling against the General are, after all, the same ones who must now deliver the new verdict and they are known as dry experts in commercial international law. If I had been one of their panel, I would have congratulated Lord Hoffmann on his ties to Amnesty, I would have proclaimed that it should be a precondition of any judge anywhere to be a member of that human rights organization. Or are we to have sitting in judgment on dictators and torturers and genocidal heads of state only those who have proven their "objectivity" by refusing to show any previous interest in crimes against humanity? Isn't that bias as well?

But of course I am not on that tribunal or any other tribunal, for that matter. A practitioner of fiction rather than of law, I am way up here in the hushed chamber that I have seen before only in movies: that plush, velvety red curtain against a backdrop of dark wooden benches, those powdered white wigs and flowing robes, the tall official who calls the session to order with several thumps of his staff carved with ancient inscriptions, reminders that this is the country that gave us the Magna Carta, the first document in history in which a ruler agreed to limits on his right to abuse his subjects—all of this adds to the dreamlike atmosphere.

Lord Browne-Wilkinson is the first to speak and—not for the first time during the session—it is not easy to understand what his verdict really is. He seems to have stated that Senator Pinochet does not have immunity and yet also—a contradiction?—he would only allow in part the appeal against the High Court's original October ruling, which did not authorize extradition proceedings.

He is followed by Lord Goff who is crystal clear. He would dismiss the appeal: Pinochet has sovereign immunity. Then comes Lord Hope of Craighead who appears to agree with Lord Goff that most of the charges alleged against Pinochet relate to crimes for which he could not be lawfully extradited, but then he reverses himself—is that what he means?—by stating that the General has no immunity, but only as regards the period after 8 December 1988. What is he talking about? Why that date? Things get more confused with Lord Hutton, the next to rise, who adds a new date, 29 September 1988. Pinochet can be extradited and tried on charges of torture and conspiracy to torture committed after that date. The next judge, Lord Saville of Newgate, agrees with Lord Browne-Wilkinson. Wait. What was it that Lord Browne-Wilkinson had said?

"What's happening?" Angélica urgently whispers to me, pulling on my jacket as if it were a piece of rope, her words making it even more difficult for my addled brain to seize and hold the slippery meaning of what is going on down there in the chamber.

"I'm trying to figure it out," I whisper back.

Diane Dixon says: "I think we're winning."

Are we?

Lord Millet then stands up and confirms this opinion. He would deny Pinochet's immunity without limitations of any sort. No dates, no ifs, no buts, in his statement. So that makes how many for and how many against? But against and for what?

The last judge rises. Lord Phillips of Worth Matravers has yet a different opinion: He would allow the appeal (against the High Court's decision to free Pinochet? Is that what he's talking about?) in respect of so much of the conduct alleged against Senator Pinochet as constitutes extradition crimes.

There is a moment of shocked silence. No murmurs, no applause, not from the conservatives who have come to see Pinochet vindicated, not from those in the human rights community who have come to see Pinochet crucified. We are all unable to cheer or jeer because, quite simply, we have not managed to quite comprehend what the hell this ruling means. Nobody moves.

The paralysis lasts only for an instant—but the instant is long and silent, full of apprehension and bafflement.

Then Lord Browne-Wilkinson acknowledges our bewilderment and explains that the condensed report of each lord may be a bit confusing—everybody laughs—and that he will explain. All ears are strained.

Most of the charges leveled against Pinochet by the government of Spain have been dismissed by a majority because they were not, at the time they were alleged to have been committed, unlawful (extraterritorial torture has only been a crime under the law of the United Kingdom from 29 September 1988). Furthermore, torture only became an international crime with universal jurisdiction, and meriting extradition, once the United Kingdom joined Spain and Chile (the other two countries involved) in signing the Torture Convention on December 8, 1988. Six to one the justices have deemed that Pinochet can be tried, therefore, for crimes committed after that date.

So the General has lost: He has no immunity and the amnesty he gave himself is invalid. On the other hand, the Law Lords have asked the home secretary to reconsider whether the extradition hearings should proceed, given the substantial reduction of extraditable charges.

What does this reduction mean? What has been left of Garzón's original 250-page indictment? Are there any crimes committed under Pinochet's last fifteen months in office (when he must have been much more careful in his methods of repression), from December 8, 1988, until March 11, 1990 (when he ceased to be president), that can be successfully proven and prosecuted and that would send him to Spain to face those charges?

On our way out, we pick up a thick set of light green pages—122 of them—that contain the detailed judgments of the Law Lords. I try to feverishly leaf through them in search of an answer to my questions. I am fortunate to have one of the English lawyers on the team supporting the Garzón accusations quickly explain to us that there are indeed—even within the limited and drastically reduced period that the Law Lords have, by a majority, allowed—cases that will lead to Pinochet's condemnation. Foremost of these is the death by torture of seventeen-year-old Marcos Quezada Yáñez, on June 24, 1989, in the small town of Curacautín. The autopsy has revealed that he died because of the beatings and electric shocks administered to him by the police as punishment for protesting Pinochet's policies. There are at least an additional twenty-eight other incidents of murder and torture that occurred after the Convention on Torture was ratified on December 8, 1988, many of them documented in the Chilean Truth and Reconciliation Report of 1991.

I leave the House of Lords into the bright London sun of Westminster and am greeted at the exit by a flock of journalists, TV cameras and photographers. I have become, somewhat reluctantly, one of those often sought out by the press to comment on the Pinochet trial, partly because of my breathless engagement in these issues, though also undoubtedly due to my command of English. It is ironic that my incessant practice of bilingualism is the direct result of my exile, of my need to survive during these long years of banishment: At the time Pinochet had come to power, I had sworn to speak only Spanish till the day I died, parading my self-enforced rejection of the English of my childhood as proof of a supposedly pure Chilean and Latin American identity. So it could be said that it was Pinochet's coup that, by sending me abroad, has landed me in my role as spokesperson. It gives me some satisfaction to think that Pinochet himself is perversely responsible for the words about to emerge from my mouth.

Yes, but what words? How to summarize—in any language—what has happened inside the House of Lords today? How to make sure that the defenders of the dictator do not entangle public opinion in nitpicking, trying to spin and obfuscate the verdict in their favor? How to speak out so that someone who is at this moment hunched over to the radio—as I have been for so many months—on the other side of the world will understand this judgment? What is the essence of what has transpired in the building I have just left, now that a second ruling has been delivered?

"Una victoria para la humanidad," I shout suddenly, waving my long scarecrow arms in the air. And then in English: "A victory for humanity, a victory for humanity."

As soon as I let out my triumphant words, I am aware that this is not merely an exhibitionistic tactic on my part to disarm our opposition. It is the wild and enthusiastic truth, it is what shines through the imbroglio of statements and dates and reservations and reductions and explanations.

We have just been blessed with a great final prize to conclude this terrible and murderous century, a decisive step forward in the quest by our species for justice and equality.

I am not exaggerating.

The question of the rights that belong to each human born on this planet due to the mere wonder of that birth, and how to insure that those rights can be defended against those who are more powerful, is clearly one of the central issues that we have grappled with since the beginning of what is called civilization, something that continues to determine the life and death of every man, woman and child on this violent Earth of ours. It is in the context of that painstaking, arduous struggle for the worth and dignity of every one of our fellows who breathe our same air that the Pinochet ruling must be placed.

It has taken humanity thousands of years to reach this moment just as it has taken us thousands of years to abolish slavery and grant rights of suffrage to everyone

Ariel Dorfman

regardless of gender or creed or skin color, just as it has taken us so long to outlaw child labor and religious discrimination, just as it seems to be taking us forever to establish that a decent wage and health care and education are rights everyone is entitled to merely because they are human. Now we are on the verge of creating a system whereby those who rule us will be held accountable, not only to their own populations, but to any court in the world that can act in their name, in the name of humanity itself.

To understand why this ruling is so momentous and monumental—effectively establishing universal jurisdiction for transgressions committed by any ruler so vast and outrageous as to qualify as a crime against the whole of mankind—requires a short detour through legal and political history.

It was in 1648 that the Peace—also known as the Treaties—of Westphalia was signed in the German towns of Münster and Osnabruck, ending eighty years of war between Spain and the Dutch, a conflagration that had devastated Europe. The signatories established sovereignty for national states (and their rulers) and therefore the elementary principle of noninterference in their internal affairs, along with the recognition of the religious rights of minorities (Catholics or Protestants in the countries where they were not a majority). This was a significant advance in its day, accepting the existence of a nation-state system that continues to this day, and regulating conflict and commerce between those nations, but it left unresolved the question of how to deal with the abuses of rulers against their own subjects. It would be 1948, exactly three hundred years later, before the United Nations—spurred into action by the atrocities of the Nazis during the Second World War (though undoubtedly the ongoing horrors of Stalinism and colonialism were also in the minds of many)—decided to adopt, on December 10 of that year, the Universal Declaration of Human Rights, which is to this day the cornerstone of the struggle for a new concept of humanity. Never before had we as a species established and demanded so many fundamental rights for every human being, never before had such a clear picture been painted of the sort of world we all aspire to, never before had the states and governments agreed to be measured by their adherence to those principles and obligations.

And never before has a piece of paper been more violated. Because that document had no enforceability. The rulers could, and did, proclaim how much they loved the words—freedom of this, freedom of that—while hiding behind nonintervention and sovereignty to do whatever they liked to their subjects (and, depending on their might, to subjects in other lands as well). The Nuremberg trials—and the less well-known but equally consequential Tokyo trials—were the first and also the last instances in which the authorities of a country (a vanquished country, of course) were tried for crimes against humanity. Since then, the twentieth century has seen a long litany of massacres and invasions, torture centers and firing squads, bombing raids and persecutions, psychiatric wards and show trials, a long litany of pain endured and justice undone. Vietnam and South Africa, Cambodia and Algiers, Prague and Buenos Aires and Beijing. Bokassa and Mengitsu, Anastasio Somoza and Ferdinand Marcos, Suharto and Saddam and Honneker and Videla, everywhere the innocent tormented and dying in ways forbidden and repudiated by the Universal Declaration of Human Rights.

Of course, conventions continued to be signed, covenants were proclaimed, protocols were debated and ratified—yes, of course, the Rights of the Child, the Elimination of All Forms of Discrimination Against Women, the Elimination of All Forms of Racial Discrimination, yes, of course, we're all against child labor and against hostage-taking, but the truth is that words are cheap and the signatories did not seem to ever expect to be called to task for their own lack of compliance with the terms of the different documents, nor were they apparently bothered by a similar incessant infringement on the part of their allies and friends around the world. Just look at Margaret Thatcher and Augusto Pinochet signing with a flourish the Convention against Torture. It is clear that the Chilean dictator never considered the remotest possibility that he could be arrested and his appeal then denied on the basis of his own autograph at the bottom of what he probably thought was no more than a few pious pages of legal gobbledygook. How could he know that he was signing his own doom, authorizing his own trial? Inconceivable that ten years later a group of Law Lords versed in commercial law would decree that a contract is a contract and is obviously supposed to be honored by those who have read, confirmed and initialed it.

But much had happened in those ten years. The most vital development was the end of the Cold War and the end, therefore, of the daily possibility of a nuclear holocaust—which had been used by the major powers to justify their own infractions and to turn a blind eye to offenses against human rights by client states. Fear of the other—Soviet fear of the West, U.S. fear of communism—had been translated into terror at home in the case of the so-called socialist countries and terror in the name of liberty abroad (and restrictions of civil liberties at home) in the case of the so-called Free World. You do whatever you want in Budapest or Tibet (though I will denounce you) as long as my boys can do whatever they want in El Salvador or Brazzaville or East Timor (though you will denounce me).

So it is not strange that the fall of the Berlin Wall was widely expected to be followed by a drastic contraction in the number of human rights violations, the creation of a world where nations could now be held up to the exacting standards of the many declarations and conventions, so that the phrase "Never again," which had burned itself into the consciousness of a humanity horrified by Auschwitz and Bergen-Belsen, could henceforth be predictive of the future rather than a mere condemnation of past misconduct.

Ariel Dorfman

Two major man-made catastrophes contradicted this optimism. The long dismemberment of Yugoslavia from 1991 onward unleashed violence and depravity on a scale not seen in Europe since the days of Nazism, of the sort reserved for the last forty years for poorer and less "civilized" zones of the world, a neocolonial brutality that was not stopped, and often perpetrated, by the Western powers. It is true that an International War Crimes Tribunal for the Former Yugoslavia had been set up in 1993 in The Hague, but like so many other initiatives it had no bite to it, did not instill alarm in the human rights violators that they would ever really be held accountable. Two years later, in 1995, at the moment when General Radovan Mladic was overseeing with relish the ethnic cleansing of Srebrenica, killing more than 7,000 Bosnian Muslims and raping their women and children under the very eyes of the United Nations peacekeepers supposed to protect them, the Court in The Hague had only one Serb torturer under arrest and had yet to try him—not a very effective form of deterrence.

The other event was an even more compelling indictment of international indifference to genocide—almost a million Tutsis murdered in Rwanda in April and May of 1994 while the Western powers and the United Nations again stood by. Naturally, yet another war crimes tribunal was created, but the persistence of such appalling collective crimes gave added momentum to the need to basically rethink how the nations of the world could generate permanent institutions to deal with outrages of this sort.

The result was that on July 17, 1998, exactly three months before Scotland Yard came calling for Pinochet, one hundred and twenty nations (but not the United States) gathered in Rome to ratify the Statute of an International Criminal Court. The agreement established mechanisms for judging rulers who have committed war crimes and crimes against humanity—but it also included the proviso that in order to surrender the accused to the organs of world justice consent was first needed by the home state. Which meant that someone like, say, Pinochet, someone who, like most retired dictators, kept enormous enclaves of power in his own country, as well as friends and cronies in privileged positions, could never be submitted to the real jurisdiction of the International Criminal Court.

Which is why the ruling of the Law Lords is so transcendental. The implementation of the Universal Declaration of Human Rights is backed by a number of national tribunals that have behind them the enforcement power of their own police forces. At the very least, this verdict will have the effect of confining former tyrants and war criminals to the borders of their own lands, afraid to venture forth into a now uncertain world. And in the best of cases, it will lead to many of them being put on trial, a warning to those who think they can maim and kill and destroy the lives of others without ever being held accountable. One more step in the age-old struggle to build one humanity, to bring justice to the world. By stripping Pinochet of his immunity, the Law

Ariel Dorfman

Lords have established a groundbreaking legal precedent that will endure beyond what may happen to his immediate person, whether he dies in London or is shipped to Madrid or is sent back home.

Not that what happens to that body is immaterial. Crimes are committed by individuals—one person gave an order to torture, another person transmitted that order, a third person put the prisoner's head inside a bag until he suffocated oh so slowly, a fourth person hid the body, a fifth person lied about the whereabouts of that body—and it is necessary, for the sake of the survivors and the victims and as a warning to present and future offenders, that punishment should be meted out. We will find out, in the days to come, if there are enough transgressions during the circumscribed period allowed by the Law Lords to keep Pinochet's extradition trial going.

It is certainly the question that gnaws at Chileans.

I find myself in front of a crew sent by Chilean National Television. A reporter asks me whether the fact that there seems to be only one case of torture left standing by the Law Lords does not mean that Pinochet's chances of being extradited have radically diminished.

I am aware that my answer will be beamed—via direct satellite—into every home in Chile.

"What if it were your mother who had died under torture?" I ask the reporter, surprised by my own vehemence. "Wouldn't you want justice to be done?"

I wait for her answer. I do not add any details about Marcos Quezada and what he must have felt when the electricity went through his body and he could not escape the pain, I do not overdramatize my question by wondering out loud what it must have meant to be there on that grill and know that you are going to die, know that nobody can save you now. Wouldn't you want justice to be done? That's all I ask. As I wait for the answer from the reporter, as I continue to wait for that answer.

•••••

The following are some of the thirty-three cases of torture in Chile that occurred after September 29 and December 8, 1988, included in the original indictment, that have now been added by Judge Balthasar Garzón in greater detail to the dossier, based on the Chilean Truth and Reconciliation Commission Report and other sources:

Jorge Antonio Marcelo SALAS ROJAS, twenty-two years old, a barber, died due to torture on September 29, 1988, in Santiago. The autopsy report specifies that the deceased presented numerous lesions all over his body: extensive blood underneath the scalp in the left back part of the skull; purple ecchymosis on the lips from small sharp blows; purple ecchymosis semicircles under the armpits; small parchmentlike plaques and excoriations on the face and ecchymosis behind the knees. There is also evidence that points to the deceased having been in contact with water, which might explain the final cause of death.

Lincoyán Nery CACERES PEÑA, sixty-one years old, married, killed by repeated blows administered by the police on May 7, 1989, in Copiapó. He had been arrested on May 4 of that year and brought to the hospital by the police, who reported that he was "suffering from an apparent attack of epilepsy." The autopsy indicated that he had died as the consequence of a cranial-encephalic traumatism with multiple fractures of the skull produced by a blunt instrument. Other detainees testified that they had heard the deceased being beaten in the next room and that he cried out many times.

Judge Garzón also adds the cases of Cecilia Magni Camino and Raúl Pellegrin Friedmann, whose bodies were found on 28 and 31 October respectively, both bodies with injuries caused by blunt instruments and showing marks of electric shocks. The cause of death of Pellegrin was asphyxiation by being under water. And on 15 December 1988, Wilson Fernando Valdebenito Juica, death by electric shock; and on December 31, 1988, Dolores Paz Cautivo Ahumada was repeatedly beaten and her sister was threatened with rape; and on 20 August and an unknown date in September 1989, Jessica Antonia Liberona Niñoles was deprived of sleep, her nine-year-old daughter was repeatedly threatened, she was interrogated while naked, and kept in dark, solitary and unsanitary conditions; and between 26 October 1989 and 1 November 1989, Marcos Paulsen Figueroa was beaten, suspended in the air, repeatedly threatened with instant death and threatened that his sisters would be tortured and sexually assaulted; and on 27 October and a date unknown in November 1989, Andrea Paulsen Figuera was deprived of sleep and water for several days and her five-year-old daughter was threatened with torture; and Claudia Varela Moya and Marcos Ariel Antonioletti Ruiz and Patricia Irarrazaval and Hernán Sepúlveda who died under torture and Jorge Muñoz who was tied up and confined in a small cage and suspended and given electric shocks and Marcelo Arturo Garay Vergara and Luis Leyton Chamorro and...

The lawyers for General Pinochet declared that all these cases are irrelevant, mere cases of ordinary police brutality, and asked that they should therefore not be taken into consideration during the extradition proceedings.

• • • • •

A few months before Pinochet was arrested, a book was published in Chile. It was written by Patricia Verdugo, the star Chilean journalist whose own father had been murdered by security forces, and transcribed the conversations held over a two-way radio between Pinochet and his fellow conspirators on September 11, 1973, as the coup progressed. I had read that transcript back in 1983 in the semi-clandestine Chilean magazine *Análsis*, but now not only was this information on sale at every newsstand in the country but one could acquire, along with it, a damning CD where we could hear Pinochet's unmistakable gruff voice. It is so different to eavesdrop on his very voice telling Admiral Carvajal that he should not accept any sort of negotiation with Allende, who was still holed up, at that hour of the morning, in La Moneda. There it was, the same voice I had heard in late August of 1973 over the phone, that same voice now shouting a few weeks later that a plane should be readied so Allende and his people can be put on it and off they go.

You can hear some doubts creeping into Carvajal's throat, unsure whether it's good to let Allende leave: "The idea is to take them prisoner for now, then we'll see," Carvajal says uncertainly. "But for now the idea is to take them prisoner."

Pinochet does not want Carvajal to think he's a sissy, so he puts his mind to rest: "My idea," says that voice I recognize as his, "is that these gentlemen [*estos caballeros*, Pinochet is always using this word ironically to refer to his adversaries] should be taken and sent by plane wherever and then when they're on their way we'll shoot the plane down."

This "idea" of Pinochet is reiterated a while later, when Carvajal suggests that Allende may want to "parlamentar," in other words, to discuss a way out of the crisis. Pinochet is very excited and barks: "Unconditional surrender! *Nada de parlamentar.* No talking things over! Unconditional surrender!"

"Good," Carvajal answers, "*muy bien, conforme.* Understood. Unconditional surrender and he's to be taken prisoner, offering nothing more than to respect his life, let's say."

"His life and his physical integrity," Pinochet says, "and then he'll be dispatched to some other place."

"Understood. So, the offer to take him out of the country still holds."

And Pinochet responds: "The offer to take him out of the country still holds. . .but the plane is going to fall, *viejo*, my friend, when it's flying away. "

And we hear Carvajal laughing at what he by now realizes is not a joke by Pinochet. Maybe getting used to Pinochet's sense of humor. And, in fact, a few hours later, when the news that Allende has been found dead in La Moneda is transmitted to Pinochet, the new ruler of Chile allows himself yet another witticism. What to do with the body? We hear Pinochet musing on whether to stick the body in a coffin and put it on a plane with the family and send it to Cuba, or whether it wouldn't be best to secretly bury it in Chile. Later I listen to those words—where he suggests turning Allende into the first *desaparecido* of Chile.

And then I hear him add a lament. "Even when he dies," Pinochet complains, "this guy is a nuisance, even dying he's causing us trouble."

There he is, our Pinochet, stripped of any statesman-like pretensions, Pinochet at his most vulgar, tasteless, coarse.

But incidents like these should not blind us, should not make us conclude that this is a man without a doctrine, a man who does not have a plan for Chile and for the world.

Two years after that September 11 conversation, in order to celebrate the second anniversary of the coup, the General delivers a televised speech in the Edificio Diego Portales establishing his thoughts on human rights, which have been used, he grumbles, as an instrument to combat "our government and our country, in every corner of the whole world."

Human rights, he says, are universal and inviolable, but not all of them can be exercised unrestrictedly nor are they of the same hierarchy. Over and over again, in this speech and many others, he uses the images of illness and cancer to explain how he understands the rights of his people. "When the social body sickens," he says, "it is not possible to enjoy every human right simultaneously. The immense majority of our fellow citizens accept and support [restrictions to human rights], because they understand that those restrictions are the price that has to be paid for tranquility, calm and social peace, that today make us into an island within a world invaded by violence, terrorism and generalized disorder."

Pinochet then explains that human rights cannot be invoked by or applied to those who want to abolish those rights, and laments that so many young people, whose parents do not share their rebellious convictions poisoned by fanaticism and hatred, need to be punished.

"As a husband and a father,' Pinochet went on to say, "I have been moved by this problem, because I understand the pain produced [by our actions] in some homes; you must believe me that for my own sensitive person it would have been far easier to yield and not to sanction [those who defy the current laws], but if I were to do so I would be betraying my duty as a ruler, given that when authority is not applied vigorously, we fall into depravity and after that into anarchy. The consequences are then paid for by all the inhabitants of the nation and end up being harsher than would have been necessary if we had decided to initially uphold public order. That is why our attitude must remain inflexible, for the good of Chile and its children."

For the good of Chile and its children.

• • • • •

It is mid-October 1999—in fact, October 14—and another momentous week has just gone by in the life of Augusto Pinochet. I have not been back to London since the March ruling at the House of Lords and yet, by a strange coincidence, I find myself once again visiting London, on my way to the Cheltenham Literary Festival, precisely in time to witness firsthand the next developments in the case. Magistrate Ronald Bartle is about to rule, after a delay of almost one year of appeals, on whether to finally find cause for the extradition hearings to begin or to send the General home due to insufficient evidence.

Outside the Bow Street Magistrate's Court, on October 8, I am once again saved from having to gather the news from the radio, once again ready to hear yet another London verdict delivered. I was not overly disappointed that this time Diane Dixon would not be able to sneak me in to the proceedings. She had hinted as much just the night before the judgment, at the Riverside Studio, when we had inaugurated an exhibition of paintings and prints by the prominent British artist Peter Griffin inspired by my poems. That event—a fund-raiser for the Victor Jara Foundation—was brimming with hundreds of friends from the English solidarity groups, along with a good sampling of Chilean expatriates and former exiles. Many of those present that night reconvened the next morning at Bow Street, having promised me that what I would be missing in dramatic suspense by not being inside when the magistrate announced his decision would be more than made up for by the very special experience of waiting for that decision on the street itself. They were right.

The Opera House of Covent Garden that faces the Magistrate's Court could not be more English: There's the Thames nearby and the enormous black taxis driving on the left and the umbrella-toting barristers, all of it quintessential London, and yet I can't shake the impression that it's all a delusion. Because what I really find myself face to face with on Bow Street is a version of Chile or, rather, a deformed mirror of the same fractured Chile whose divided camps have been confronting each other over the last decades. I find myself transported back to my country without having to leave London. On one flank of the courthouse (and massed in front of it) are the innumerable members of the *Piquete de Londres*, who continue their yearlong incessant protests and wild drum beatings and chants. But they are not alone. On the opposite side of the street, protected by a phalanx of imposing bobbies, a group of Pinochetistas hold up banners and placards ("Gracias, General"; "Return our Savior to Chile"), trying somewhat fruitlessly to make their voices heard over the infernal din. These other Chileans— mostly well-to-do women—have been flown in from Santiago on tours organized by the Pinochet Foundation, an attempt to instruct the world with their version of how the General saved them from world communism. One of the jokes that circulates is that these "Pinotours" are remarkably expensive because the voyagers have to pay for two tickets: one for the lady of the house in business class and another in coach for the maid that is accompanying her. But the insults that the two groups hurl at each other are no laughing matter. Nor is the red paint that some distraught members of the *Piquete* try to spatter on right-wing Chilean politicians as they enter the courthouse. One agitated young man dressed like a skeleton manages to jump the police lines and spit on slim, well-dressed Evelyn Matthei, a venomous Chilean senator who has come to London to accompany the General in his hour of need. I admit to feeling slightly embarrassed, almost affronted, at the zeal and hysteria of the two groups.

For the first time since Pinochet has been arrested, I would rather not have the eyes of the world watching us,

I would rather conceal from the rest of the planet the raw nakedness of our mutual hatred, this lack of even the semblance of a dialogue. Or is this inevitable? When you expose your dictator to the judgment of humanity, can you avoid exposing your own failings and weaknesses as well, the tangled country that he is bequeathing to us? Aren't we, after all as imprisoned in Pinochet's cage as he is in ours, disputing his image and his legacy?

That verdict is taking its time in coming—and the crowd is getting more upset and roiled by the minute. There are rumors that on this occasion the ruling will favor the General. Magistrate Bartle is a close acquaintance of Margaret Thatcher and has a reputation as a staunch conservative. In fact, banking on that possible decision against the demand for extradition, the Spanish government had in the last weeks mounted a diplomatic maneuver to block any possible appeal by Garzón, so that Pinochet could go free immediately. That stratagem had been discovered and nipped in the bud—but its mere existence suggests that the English magistrate will conclude that the Crown lawyers speaking for Garzón have not proven their case.

It turns out that our apprehensions—and the high hopes of the Spanish government of José María Aznar and the clamorous Pinotourists shouting outside the Bow Street courthouse—are misplaced. When the verdict arrives, it is an even stronger indictment of the General than anything that has been pronounced in any English court thus far. Bartle has found that the tortures inflicted upon the victims were not isolated cases but part of a systematic and deliberate conspiracy to terrorize the country at large. And he has not only declared that there are more than enough reasons to allow the extradition to proceed, making it harder for Pinochet's attorneys to disprove the evidence that has just been admitted, but this conservative judge has also agreed to consider in the upcoming trial a series of crimes against humanity that go far beyond the scope allowed by the Law Lords in their recent restricted determination.

What this means, as I come to realize during the ensuing days while reading Bartle's decision, is that Garzón need not limit the evidence he is presenting to the English courts to the fate of the victims of torture during Pinochet's last year and a half in office, but may add all the unresolved cases of disappearances in Chile since the coup itself. Those men and women who were abducted so many years ago and whose bodies are still missing constitute, according to Bartle, an ongoing violation of the law, a crime which has not ended and for which Pinochet is therefore still, at this very moment, responsible. The English magistrate has even appended a special paragraph about the suffering of the relatives of the disappeared and how the unusual cruelty of the perpetual punishment inflicted upon them should also be taken into account during the extradition hearings.

What is interesting about this noteworthy part of the ruling is that it echoes the reasoning refined and advanced by Chilean judge Juan Guzmán Tapia, who, back in Santiago, has since January 20, 1998, been patiently investigating a series of disappearances under Pinochet's reign, refusing to apply the amnesty or immunity to the former president. Like Magistrate Bartle, Judge Guzmán considers that Pinochet can be charged with kidnapping, a crime that will not cease until the bodies of the missing are produced, dead or alive.

And why does it matter, what a lonely judge in Chile may be doing or dreaming of doing? Isn't his pursuit of the General an exercise in futility, if Pinochet's fate will be decided here in London and later in Madrid? Hasn't this latest verdict guaranteed that the former dictator will not be able to avoid his eventual extradition to Spain?

In effect, that is the Chilean government's conclusion: The legal challenges to that extradition have been exhausted or will be met with one refusal after the other, and so the time has most definitely come to try something else. A mere six days after Bartle's ruling, on this fourteenth day of October 1999, the English press carries the news that the minister of foreign affairs of Chile has asked the Blair government to submit General Augusto Pinochet—soon to be eighty-four years old—to medical exams to determine if his ill health and frail memory make him unable to stand trial and therefore warrant his immediate return to Santiago. By sidestepping the judicial process and focusing on the infirmity and indisposition of the accused, the Chileans hope to give Jack Straw, the minister of home affairs, a dignified way of sending the General home without appearing to interfere in the pursuit of justice. After all, even those of us who dream of General Pinochet confronting his victims one by one in a Madrid courtroom have to reluctantly admit that if this culprit (or any other one) does not possess full consciousness, it would be senseless to submit him to prosecution. What would be judged in that room is a mere husk of a man, the outward trappings of a mindless human being, and no longer effectively Pinochet himself.

It is not clear if this diplomatic offensive by the Chilean authorities to declare Pinochet unfit to stand trial will succeed, but there are signs that we are only now going to see true international pressure fully applied. Not that the present government of President Eduardo Frei has ever considered the arrest of Pinochet as anything other than an unmitigated disaster for Chile. Many of the government's own supporters on the left enthusiastically endorse Pinochet's trial abroad, creating a source of ceaseless tension within the Concertación, the government coalition. The fact that some members of Congress belonging to the Concertación have even gone to London to give evidence against Pinochet—most notably Isabel Allende, the daughter of the former president (not to be confused with the novelist), and Juan Pablo Letelier, the son of Allende's murdered minister of defence and foreign Affairs—and been refused the use of the very Chilean Embassy where the right wingers have received a warm greeting has almost led to the withdrawal of the Socialists from the government. As to that

Ariel Dorfman

right-wing opposition, it has used Chile's international humiliation and loss of sovereignty to wrap itself in the rhetoric of ultranationalism and attack the government for its inability to stand up for the fatherland. And the more fascistic elements in the military have been emboldened, interrupting the slow process of coaxing the armed forces back into their barracks after two decades of political activism and interference in civilian affairs. And, of course, the auspicious and thriving case against Pinochet in England and Spain (France and Belgium and Switzerland have also lodged arrest warrants) brings into even starker relief the weakness and craven timidity with which the democratic governments treated the General and his cohorts.

This ongoing crisis has recently been worsened by upcoming presidential elections. For the first time since Allende's thousand days, another Socialist, albeit a more lukewarm one, is the candidate of the Concertación in the election to be held in December of this year. It is a test of Chile's return to democracy that the Socialist Ricardo Lagos, a prominent member of Allende's government and an atheist to boot, can be accepted as a candidate for head of state and not be vetoed by the army or sabotaged by the business community. Lagos, who was jailed under the dictatorship and became famous for confronting Pinochet publicly, is fighting a difficult campaign against an extremely well-financed populist right-wing candidate, Joaquin Lavin. Pinochet's arrest has allowed Lavin, once a rabid supporter, to distance himself from the former dictator, an operation of obfuscation that would not be as easy to perform if the General were to return home. Is this the last service, then, that Pinochet will perform for his disciples, his very absence the paradoxical condition that will lead to a return to power of those followers?

No, there is another service of another sort by Pinochet to his cause that the Concertación government fears even more, and that has given its new diplomatic offensive an urgency it had not shown up till now. What does the right wing expect Pinochet to do?

To die abroad. That's what.

That would be enough, according to many analysts, to turn him into a martyr and a victim, transformed by the monopolistic right-wing Chilean press into a hero who perished in a foreign jail upholding the right of the father-land to be sovereign, the last sacrifice of a life dedicated to the common folk who turned their back on him but who will one day recognize his greatness, *el General de los pobres*, the General of the poor, as he likes to present himself. What better scenario for the conservatives in Chile: Pinochet's death abroad erasing all the crimes he committed at home, his ghost obliterating the ghosts of the missing he has forced to wander in search of burial?

"If he dies in England or Spain, we will never be rid of him," a friend of mine very high up in the Frei government tells me when I call him from London to discuss these matters. "If we can bring him back, there is now a real chance that he could be judged in Chile."

I am doubtful that Pinochet could, in fact, be put on trial in Chile, even now. In the midst of the electoral campaign, many prominent former Pinochet supporters have had to announce that the courts in Chile rather than those in Spain or England should resolve this matter, and those very courts are beginning to show, for the first time in over two decades, real independence, refusing—for instance—to apply the Pinochet amnesty to cases dealing with the disappeared and also taking these lawsuits away from military tribunals. But it remains to be seen whether this will amount to much if Pinochet effectively returns to Santiago. I don't envisage the army standing by idly while its former Commander in Chief is finger-printed, placed under house arrest, arraigned in court. Whereas in Spain or England it would have no way of pressuring judges, government, police, public opinion. So it seems to me self-evident that if we are to get a measure of justice, some guarantee of a fair trial, this would have to be abroad and not back home.

As Jack Straw readies a cluster of doctors to examine the old despot, I catch myself, for the first time since that day so far in the past when I heard Pinochet's voice on the phone, wishing that our General should live a long and healthy life. May those physicians find him sound in body and sane in mind, tell us that his heart will beat for many years and his faculties are as sharp as they were when he ordained the death of so many of my friends.

May Pinochet live many years.

• • • • •

Excerpts from a statement by British Home Secretary Jack Straw on Thursday, March 2, 2000:

"I have today decided that I will not order the extradition of Senator Pinochet to Spain. I made this decision under section 12 of the Extradition Act of 1989. I have also decided not to issue Authorities to Proceed in respect of extradition requests from Switzerland, Belgium and France....

"On 11 January 2000, the Secretary of State informed those acting for Senator Pinochet and the Kingdom of Spain that he had commissioned a medical report on Senator Pinochet, which had been delivered to the Home Office on 6 February 2000. He informed them that the report indicated that Senator Pinochet was unfit to stand trial, and that no significant improvement to that position could be expected...

"On 14 October 1999, shortly after the decision of the Magistrate [Bartle] to commit Senator Pinochet, the Secretary of State received through diplomatic channels representations from the Chilean Embassy, supported by medical reports, which suggested that there had been a recent and significant deterioration in Senator Pinochet's health.... He therefore decided to invite Senator Pinochet to submit to a medical examination by a team of clinicians appointed by him. The object was to obtain an independent, comprehensive and authoritative report on the relevant clinical facts....

Ariel Dorfman

"The critical facts [of the original report] are as follows:

"The clinicians...concluded that Senator Pinochet would not at present be mentally capable of meaningful participation in a trial, on the basis of: (i) Senator Pinochet's memory deficit for both recent and remote events; (ii) his limited ability to comprehend complex sentences and questions owing to memory impairment and a consequent inability to process verbal information appropriately; (iii) his impaired ability to express himself audibly, succinctly and relevantly; and (iv) easy fatigability.

"With these impediments, Senator Pinochet would be unable to follow the process of a trial sufficiently to instruct Counsel. He would have difficulty in understanding the content and implications of questions put to him and would have inadequate insight into this difficulty....

"The disabilities identified in the medical report are due to widespread brain damage, the major episodes of which seem to have occurred during September and October 1999 when Senator Pinochet suffered a number of strokes....

"The clinicians considered that further deterioration in both his physical and mental condition was likely to occur.... They have [further] advised the Secretary of State that there was no evidence that Senator Pinochet was trying to fake disability.... It is important to point out that the outward manner of Senator Pinochet is not *necessarily a reliable guide to his mental condition. It is characteristic of persons with a high level of original intelligence that they are able to mask superficially a significant impairment of cognitive functions...*

"The Secretary of State is advised that the attempted trial of an accused in the condition diagnosed in Senator Pinochet. . .could not be a fair trial in any country and would violate Article 6 of the European Convention of Human Rights in those countries which are party to it."

• • • • •

And so, the old fox has outwitted us yet one more time.

On this third day of March of the year 2000, I watch General Augusto Pinochet rolled out of the airplane that has flown him from London, I watch General Pinochet arriving in Chile after seventeen months of house arrest, one month for each year of his regime, I tell myself, as if this correlation of numbers and magical equivalences somehow constitutes a sign that there is some abstruse balance of justice in a universe that has allowed the dictator to escape punishment.

Is this how our dreams end? With a dictator who flees a rainy England at dawn and a bulky Chilean Air Force jet that hastily lifts off before the victims can file one last appeal and a mid-Atlantic refueling stop in the Ascension Islands, the only territory between London and Santiago that is under British jurisdiction, the only place where Interpol cannot arrest the General if he touches down? Is

Ariel Dorfman

that our consolation, that Pinochet is, at least, restricted to his own land from now on, that he will never again travel to visit his tailor on Bond Street?

I am watching Pinochet's return to Chile on my computer screen here in North Carolina, the web bringing me this live stream of images that a television station is transmitting from the Santiago airport.

The brass band begins to play a German marching song—how Pinochet loves those songs that were brought to our army by the Prussian officers who made it into an efficient killing machine in the nineteenth century!—as the wheelchair descends onto Chilean soil. Well, not the soil, not yet, because Pinochet is being lowered onto an ostentatiously red carpet reserved for foreign dignitaries and heads of state, absolutely inappropriate for a fugitive from justice. The whole welcoming ceremony, in fact, can be seen as a provocation, as it apparently has not been approved by any civilian authorities—who are noticeably absent. The Commander in Chief of the Chilean Army, General Ricardo Izurieta, now approaches Pinochet, who looks up and recognizes his host and then suddenly, yes, he stands up, he rises triumphantly from his confinement and gives Izurieta an *abrazo*, and then lifts an arm in the air and with the other on his walking stick, begins to walk, with relatively firm steps, reviewing the troops that offer him a salute as if he were a hero returning from a victorious battlefield while the band strikes up yet another German marching song. Now Pinochet greets his family one by one, with hugs, while a crowd of supporters who have been waiting for hours outside the airport shout themselves hoarse, and he turns in their direction and lifts both his arms in salute, before he is hustled into a helicopter, on his way, according to a TV commentator, to the official military hospital where he will be submitted to exams and where yet another group of cohorts awaits him with still more fervorous chants and hymns. The webcast shows me the streets of the Barrio Alto of Santiago—the affluent neighborhoods closer to the mountains—where the houses are bedecked with Chilean flags and florid matrons are crying in gratitude at the liberation of their leader.

It is frustrating to watch all this, of course. Till the last moment, it seemed as if those who wanted Pinochet extradited would be able to stop his return. For the last two months there have been a series of intricate maneuvers to challenge Straw's decision and the medical report. Eminent neurologists in England, distinguished psychiatrists in Madrid and in Chile and from around the world, have lodged their own reports, explaining in excruciating detail (and convincingly, according to my admittedly prejudiced opinion) how the team that reported to the British home secretary had made extensive medical mistakes that completely invalidated the claim that Pinochet was unfit to stand trial. Not one of these exhaustive critiques was admitted as evidence because Spain refused to appeal Straw's decision. Even so, for a while it almost seemed as if Pinochet would at the last moment be retained for one more year. Along with six human rights groups, Belgium (a country that has increasingly become the most vocal of contemporary nations in the fight against impunity, due to a recent law that gives its courts jurisdiction to pursue cases of genocide anywhere in the world that they might occur) managed to get three High Court judges to agree to a full judicial review of Straw's decision. But that possibility fizzled out and other last-minute legal scrambles to keep the General in England also misfired.

According to an article by Jamie Wilson in today's *London Guardian*, it appears that we were deluded to even think that Pinochet would stay in England. In fact, the fix has been in for several months. At a secret meeting in June of 1999 between British Foreign Secretary Robin Cook and his Spanish counterpart Abel Matutes during a summit in Rio, they agreed that things had already gone too far. Cook is reported to have said about Pinochet: "I will not let him die in Britain," and Matutes to have replied: "I will not let him come to Spain." So that when Juan Gabriel Valdés, Chile's foreign minister, at a meeting at the UN in September, suggested to Cook that the deterioration of the General's condition was the way of easing Pinochet back home, the deal was sealed.

Maybe I should have realized it when, over the course of the last year, photos of Pinochet's hands began to surface in the press, naked and trembling and brittle. I felt a certain satisfaction at those shaky and decrepit hands being exposed to the voyeurs of the world, I noted that those hands were now asking for mercy, I told myself that at least the trial had stripped those hands of the gloves, forced them out of hiding. But it was all a strategy, a ploy for public sympathy, a public relations ruse.

Watching his helicopter take off into the hazy blue sky of Santiago, become a dot on the screen, I ask myself once again if I have come any closer to resolving the enigma of Pinochet—which is, after all, the enigma of how so much evil can originate in someone who seems offensively ordinary and even mediocre? So many pathological reports on his mind, so many tests that doctors and psychiatrists and specialists have administered to him during the last months, so many charts and elucidations and diagnoses, and nothing to indicate the all-important question of how an intellect becomes malignant.

Oh to be able to get inside those thoughts of his, those memories, get in there through the back door, almost unawares, and register what he knows, what he silenced in himself while he spoke to me with that voice I heard on the phone back in La Moneda when Allende was still alive, what he was secretly commanding with a flick of the hand he waved at me that day in Santiago on my forlorn street corner ten years later in 1983.

I have the suspicion—though not the certainty—that Pinochet, whose mind Jack Straw has declared too feeble to comprehend what is happening to him, is still entirely and astutely his own self, in other words, someone who remembers clearly who he is and exactly what he did and what orders he uttered. I do not doubt that he can answer quite simple questions such as, What did you eat for breakfast this morning? And while we're on the subject of breakfasts, do you remember sharing a morning meal each dawn with General Manuel Contreras, the head of your secret police, one hour and a half each day for years and years? During so many hours and so many cups of coffee, did you ever speak, even once, of the disappearances of the opponents to your regime? Not curious about them at all? Did you never mention, while you chewed on your toast and jam, what was happening in the dark cellars that Contreras reigned over? The howls that spilled out of those cellars with such intensity that people in the streets thought twice before daring to rebel or resist?

These questions and so many others are still awaiting a response and what everybody is wondering now is whether, given that they will not be asked in Spain, is there still a possibility that extensive answers could be demanded in Chile itself? After all, the Chilean government has incessantly insisted that conditions exist to bring General Pinochet to trial in his fatherland and we will now find out if those statements were sincere or a mere tactic to get Pinochet liberated. The signals are mixed. Ricardo Lagos, elected the first Socialist president of Chile since Allende by a thin margin, has just declared that justice needs to be done, though other members of his coalition have said that if foreign doctors have excused Pinochet from the tribulations of due process abroad, it seems obvious that for the same reasons he could not be subjected to a trial in Chile. The right wing seems equally divided, with some of its conservative lawmakers already backpedaling from their ostentatious assurances that Pinochet had to be tried in his own country, while others, noticeably Joaquín Lavín, the presidential candidate who polled 48 percent of the vote in the recent elections, continue to try to distance themselves from the former dictator.

The camera switches to the Association of Relatives of the Disappeared, who have been holding an all-night candlelight vigil. Viviana Díaz, whose father, Victor, was taken from her twenty-eight years ago and never seen again, tells a reporter that this is a farce. They had warned the world that Pinochet would try to fool the British home secretary and now he is making a mockery of everyone who believed in his illness. But he is returning, Viviana adds, as a criminal. So we are going to demand justice. He is going to be put on trial here in Chile.

Is she right? Can my dream still come true? Or has my own mind grown feverish, consoling myself with the fantasy of a non-existent future world where nobody is above the law?

A bit later in the day, however, a wire from Santiago transmits a statement from Judge Juan Guzmán, who presently has fifty-nine cases open against Pinochet (with one or two more being added every day as relatives come forward to press charges): "I believe," the judge says, "that the conditions are in place for the development of a good trial in our country and from next Monday I will dedicate myself exclusively to this end."

Of course, in order to even be able to begin that monumental task, he must first seek to divest the General of his parliamentary immunity, proving to a court of appeals and eventually to the Chilean Supreme Court that there is sufficient evidence of criminal behavior to warrant such a drastic measure against a sitting member of the Senate. It is to that Supreme Court where our attention will turn in the next months and perhaps years, wondering about the opinions and secret alliances among its members, somewhat in the way in which we became experts in the previous rulings of hitherto unknown English barristers, magistrates and Law Lords.

There have been notable changes in the Chilean judiciary. The Supreme Court was, for far too long, a bastion of Pinochet support—greeting the coup against Allende with alacrity; refusing to accept habeas corpus writs on behalf of the *desaparecidos*; turning a blind eye to outrages that could have been investigated and maybe even mitigated; and, as recently as August of 1990, at a time when Commander in Chief of the Army Pinochet was warning that if anybody touched one of his men there would be serious consequences, unanimously declaring the Amnesty Law of 1978 to be constitutional, which meant that lower courts were forbidden from even inquiring into disappearances. And one year later, in 1991, the Court punished Judge Carlos Cerda with a two-month suspension without pay because he refused to apply the amnesty law to a case of thirteen missing citizens. And in 1993 it declined to investigate the Prats case. And in 1994 that same Supreme Court closed the case of the Spanish diplomat Carmelo Soria, murdered in 1976 by Pinochet agents who had confessed to the crime. And in 1995 it agreed that the General could bring a lawsuit against Arturo Barrios, a former university student leader who had publicly declared that the tyrant should be put on trial for human rights violations during the military dictatorship (Barrios was subsequently jailed). And then in 1997 the Supreme Court justices asked the lower Chilean courts to quickly resolve and dispatch any pending human rights accusations by applying the amnesty law. A shameful history of genuflection to the power of the state past and present.

Even so, appointments by the two democratic presidents have begun, albeit gradually, to build a potentially independent judiciary. By the end of 1997, the Supreme Court, for the first time decides to reverse the application of Pinochet's amnesty law and, in a separate ruling, doesn't allow a military tribunal to close other cases. Decisions of this sort begin to occur more frequently once the General ceases to command the army and becomes Senator for Life, and really gather steam from the moment that Pinochet is arrested in London, with more and more new cases introduced against significant numbers of former (and a couple of active) members of the armed forces. More crucially, a series of cases that had been closed due to the amnesty law are reopened—worrying members of the military, the army in particular, which foresees an endless number of debilitating lawsuits.

Ariel Dorfman

This fresh openness toward investigations has been called a "new doctrine" by the Supreme Court—and some of its members have ruled that not only should the crimes be scrutinized but that even if they were committed during the period recognized by the amnesty law, that law cannot be applied anyway as it violates international treaties that Chile had signed, such as the Geneva Convention (on the treatment of prisoners of war). The question is if this momentum will last now that Pinochet is home. Perhaps now that there is no longer any need to prove to the world that Chilean judges are independent enough to put the General and his henchmen on trial, the impetus for judicial activism will fizzle. Or will the pressure remain on the Chilean courts to carry out their promises? Will the eyes of the world stay glued to what happens in my country to see how all this ends, this story that opened with a raid by Scotland Yard in London in October 1998 and whose final act is still being written elsewhere? Or does nobody care anymore about the outcome of this process, now that it has been banished to the distant outskirts of human history, now that it does not involve Madrid and London and Washington, now that Pinochet has been thrust back upon us as a burden that others have had enough of?

He's your monster. You deal with him.

But isn't this what I have been hoping for? Praying for? Now that the General has helped the people of the world establish the groundbreaking precedent that a head of state can be judged for crimes against humanity by any court in the world acting in the name of that wounded humanity, are we not being given an extraordinary opportunity, the chance to put him on trial all over again, now in our own soiled backyard? Of course his escape, no matter how ignominious and grotesque, leaves a certain bitter aftertaste, the realization that all men are not treated equally by the law, that someone like Pinochet is given special dispensations and privileges. So what else is new?

Chile's sovereignty, invoked so tediously by the government, is about to receive its true test. Sovereignty means subordinating the armed forces which will resist seeing the man who led them for twenty-five years treated as an ordinary citizen. Sovereignty means that the Pinochetistas, a minority in the country according to every free election and every poll ever taken, should not be allowed to block our democracy. Sovereignty must mean sovereignty over our past.

Because the *Jefe Máximo* did not act alone.

There are many, far too many, who participated in these crimes. Starting, of course, with the hundreds of military personnel and their civilian acolytes, who carried out the General's orders, the men who pulled the trigger or plunged the knife or attached the metal clasp. Not to mention those who bought the materials with which those horrors were perpetrated, those who kept the accounts and balanced the budget for the purchases, those who rented the basements and cleaned them out, those who paid the agents' salaries and typed out the reports and confessions and served the coffee and cookies when the warriors wearied of their epic task. And then there are the others, the less visible others by the thousands who denied those transgressions were being visited on their compatriots, knowing full well what was happening, or justifying them as a sort of "collateral damage" unfortunately necessary to tame the barbarian Marxist hordes.

As I turn off the computer, not wanting, not needing, to watch the scene where jubilant fascist multitudes greet their returning hero with joy under the strong summer sun of Santiago, I think of yet others. Those who shut their eyes in order not to see, those who decided to ignore the howls, those who murmured at home and often in more public places that the mothers of the missing were crazy, *unas locas*, what those women need is a good fuck. And those who used the dictatorship as an opportunity to get rich, to buy the public enterprises at scandalously low prices, to fire any worker who might show the slightest sign of insubordination. And others: those who, later on, when democracy arrived, preferred to forget, preferred amnesia and frenetic consumption while pain was dismissed to the alleyways of our land, while pain leaked out of the mind and memory of our land. So many who, by their silence, allowed Pinochet to prosper, Pinochet to exist.

All those who, if Pinochet is judged, would have to ask themselves: Up to what point am I responsible for the lack of justice in my country? What am I ready to do in order to remedy this predicament?

Pinochet is a mirror. Are we really ready to judge him?

It is a question we need to ask ourselves, whatever may happen to the perishable body or the cunning or deteriorated mind of the man who ruled our destiny for so many years. With or without immunity, with or without a trial.

Are we willing to judge the country that gave origin to Pinochet?

It is this question and this ultimate looking glass that the General brings us, like a perverse and marvelous gift, from the world beyond our borders.

Maybe this dream has, in fact, just begun,

• • • • •

"What would you think if there's a bomb in a hospital and you know that What's-his-name, some guy, has information about where that bomb is located? And he says to you: 'I'm not telling you a thing, because I don't know anything.' What do you do? I'm asking you right now: can you justify, can you accept, that the person says, 'I don't know where the bomb is,' and you know that innocent people are going to die there and that there's no time to evacuate the sick? Are you going to just wait around until the bomb explodes?"

Words spoken by Pinochet in an interview in 1989.

How many times have we seen this argument used, how many times have you heard someone suggest that perhaps, at some point, who knows, even the most civilized among us might be willing to torture a suspect,

Ariel Dorfman

bomb innocent civilians, or restrict a defendant's right to a lawyer or a fair trial, all in the name of saving the innocent?

Maybe what is frightening about Pinochet is not how far from us he has been all this time, but how very close. Just a stone's throw away. Such a short distance that separates him from ordinary human beings who would never in their lives dream of really hurting somebody else.

Maybe my need to exorcise him, to put him on trial, is really the need to banish that closeness, set him apart from the rest of humanity, punish in him what we fear we might also do, we might be horribly tempted to do, may the Lord help us, under the wrong circumstances.

● ● ● ● ●

Friends die and when their death has been violently inflicted by the state it may often take many years to find out where it transpired, and at times it may even take longer to find out how and why.

That was the case with Carlos Berger.

Although I had run into his widow, Carmen Hertz, in Buenos Aires in the early months of 1974—both of us in the first stages of our exile—I can't recall ever having heard from her the details of how her husband had been murdered by the military in Calama. Maybe she wasn't talking, maybe I wasn't asking, maybe we had other things on our mind—like fleeing Argentina before we got killed by the death squads that were already starting to operate there. Or maybe if Carlos had been one of my closest friends…. But he was, like so many of my compañeros of that time, someone I had come to know intermittently over the years. I might have met him during my adolescence, as my parents knew his Communist parents, particularly Dora Guralnik, his mother, but my first nebulous memories of him are at the University of Chile where he studied law and I did literature, and then I can indistinctly recall him and Carmen during the frenetic presidential campaigns of the sixties. I finally got to know him a bit better during the thousand days of Salvador Allende, as one of my multiple jobs was to help bring out Onda, a pop culture juvenile magazine at Quimantú, the state publishing house, which competed healthily for the youth market with Ramona, a publication which Carlos directed. We talked often, and heatedly, about how the media could help liberate minds instead of drowning them in cultural garbage and how challenging it was to attempt this in a revolution that fully respected the democratic rights of the opposition. I liked his sense of humor, and his intense, almost fierce, political conviction that combined curiously with a certain laid-back quality, a stubbornness that did not preclude tolerance for opposing points of view. Once he left that job, I had run into him a couple of times—he was working as a journalist at the Ministry of Finance and that's where I assumed the military takeover had caught him. So it came as a shock sometime in late October 1973 to read in the newspapers—by then I had sought asylum in the Argentine

Embassy and was waiting for a safe-conduct pass to leave Chile—that, branded as a "Communist terrorist," he had been shot in the north of the country while trying to escape from a military squadron.

It was a lie, of course. But how much of a lie I only found out in 1989, in the final months of the Pinochet government when I read an extraordinary book, Los Zarpazos del Puma, in which the Chilean journalist Patricia Verdugo—yes, the same fearless reporter who published the transcript of Pinochet's secret conversations during the coup—revealed to hundreds of thousands of readers the story of the Caravana de la Muerte, the Caravan of Death, that had taken the lives of seventy-five innocent men, Carlos Berger among them. Strangely enough, by then Angélica and I had grown much closer to Carmen Hertz and yet, perhaps out of a natural sense of discretion between friends, had still not heard from her lips how Carlos had died.

Less than a month before Allende's overthrow, they had moved, with their eight-month-old son, Germán, to Calama so that Carlos could direct the local radio station El Loa—and that's where the coup found him on the morning of September 11, 1973. For refusing the military command to shut down the radio's transmissions, he was arrested that same day and then released later that night, only to be detained again in a brutal raid a bit before dawn on September 12. He was tried by a military tribunal and Major Fernando Reveco sentenced him to sixty-one days in jail for continuing to broadcast, a mild verdict in those terrible times. This sentence and many others that Reveco pronounced against other Allende supporters proved so mild, in fact, that in early October he was relieved of his command, sent to Santiago, interrogated and tortured by his own comrades-in-arms and then jailed for two years before being banished, a fate shared by several other officers in other parts of Chile who had shown restraint during the military takeover.

October 19, 1973, was supposed to be a happy day for Carlos. Just the day before, Carmen—who was a lawyer—had convinced a military officer that, given that her husband had served half his term and had shown exemplary conduct, the rest of the sentence could be commuted for a fine, and a deal had been agreed to. She had even bought two airplane tickets so both of them could fly to Santiago the following morning.

But October 19 was also the day when a Puma helicopter of the Chilean Army landed in Calama. Out stepped General Sergio Arellano Stark in full battle gear, accompanied by several officers whose names, unfortunately, would resurface over and over again in one accusation after the other through the years, officers who would form the backbone of the DINA, the special secret police unit created by Manuel Contreras at the behest of General Pinochet. Officers like Lieutenant Colonel Pedro Espinoza, who would be the second in command of DINA and the head of the torture camp of Tejas Verdes. And Colonel Sergio Arredondo, who would later be military attaché to Brazil, where he coordinated the *foreign secret police operations of the five countries involved in Operation Condor. And Lieutenant Armando Fernández Larios, who had reportedly led the assault on La Moneda and would later be accused and convicted of several DINA operations in Chile and abroad, including the confessed murder of Spanish diplomat Carmelo Soria in Santiago and of Orlando Letelier and Ronni Moffit in Washington. And Major Marcelo Moren Brito, who was to be in charge of the clandestine torture center of Villa Grimaldi, where witnesses have placed most of those prisoners who were later to be among the* desaparecidos *from throughout the entire nation during the regime.*

The purported mission of this high-level, carefully selected group of officers was to review the War Council proceedings for political prisoners and standardize procedures—but what that really meant had been revealed by the visits of the retinue to other cities. Taking off from Santiago's Tobabalaba airport on September 30, Arellano and company had gone first south and then north. In each city where there had been no sentences and no political prisoners, the commanding officer had been relieved and, later, arrested and sent to Santiago; and in cities where there had been military tribunals but the results had been judged to be lenient or compassionate, a series of prisoners already serving sentences had been illegally hauled out of their cells and executed.

Calama was the last stop of an itinerary of mayhem. Cauquenes on October 4: Four prisoners killed. That same day in Valdivia: Twelve prisoners shot. October 16, La Serena: Fifteen prisoners are abducted from the local jail and executed, among them Jorge Peña, who had created the first orchestra in Chile entirely formed by children. That same night, the Caravana forcibly removed thirteen men from the city jail of Copiapó and executed them in a sector called Cuesta Cardones, accusing the dead of having tried to escape custody. On October 18, it is Antofagasta's turn: Fourteen prisoners are taken to the Quebrada El Way and murdered there (among them is Eugenio Ruiz Tagle, a name we will come across again).

And then, Arellano and his brigade arrived in Calama.

By three o'clock in the afternoon, when Carmen came to see Carlos in jail to tell him that apparently the agreement to free him had fallen through, for reasons that she could not yet fully understand, she found him nervous and very worried. Half the prisoners had been taken from the jail a few hours before, their faces hooded and their hands tied behind their back, taken off for what the authorities said was an interrogation. Carmen stayed with Carlos until five o'clock and then left him there. Her last memory of him is that he was nicely toasted by the sun and she remembers his blue jeans and his shirt and his pipe and the last kiss he gave her.

By six, Carlos was dead—though Carmen was not to know this till much later. Witnesses who began to come forward over the years declare that he was taken, along with twenty-five other detainees to a mountainous zone called Topater, not far from Chuquicamata, which was

Ariel Dorfman

then and still is today the largest open-pit copper mine in the world. I have been there, in that desert, I have visited that mine in the Atacama desert, one the driest expanses of sand and rock in the world. That's where Carlos and the others were executed by the men who had come with General Arellano. According to local soldiers and officers who had been asked to assist and were horrified at what they watched, the executions were not quick. The members of the Caravan of Death took their time, shooting the prisoners in the legs first and then aiming at other parts of their bodies and then mutilating them with long knives called corvos, scooping out the eyes and defacing each man and forcing the other prisoners to observe the fate that was awaiting them. Only thirteen corpses of the twenty-six were returned to their families for burial, perhaps because the others had been so grievously defiled, perhaps for some other reason we may never know. At any rate, the other bodies were disappeared and are still, to this day, missing. Among them was the body that had once housed Carlos Berger, the hands that had once written the following letter to his wife on September 26, 1973, from the Calama jail:

"My darling and adored little woman: It will never be possible to reproduce the anguish and the oppression that we have felt when our sentences were announced to us. Just imagine. The names are called out one by one. And they come back up to the cells. They come in and say: eight years. It's the turn of X to go down. A frightening silence ensues and the new one goes down from the cell. A while later, he comes up and says: 'They hit me with fifteen years. Z should go down.' And that's how it goes, repeating the same thing each time. Sentences of five hundred and six hundred days, eight, fifteen, sixteen, twenty-five years. It was enough to make you want to cry. But the guys really stood up to the test. Bitter and screwed up, of course, but full of dignity. That's when I missed you most. I wasn't part of the sentencing, but I felt depressed anyway and that's when one feels the need to speak to somebody and that somebody couldn't be anybody but you...

"Now it's almost noon on Thursday. They've informed me of my final sentence: sixty days in prison in Calama.... Well, that means I get to spend a season here, enjoying the sun, sports, the water with traces of arsenic. I hope they'll respect the norm that takes into account time already served, with which I'd already have almost fifteen days of my sentence done. I hope you come today in the afternoon. I adore you. Carlos. And how I love that little blonde dwarf of ours."[3]

Carlos never suspected, of course, while writing that letter, that Carmen would have to bring up their son by herself, Or of her exile with little Germán and the complicated return to Chile and how it took that son of theirs most of his life to dare to visit the Calama desert where his father had been killed. Nor could Carlos have anticipated what would happen to his own parents, the silent victims whose names are not on the memorial in the cemetery in Santiago. Carlos could not have known,

I hope he did not divine, that his father, Julio Berger, fighting chronic depression, would commit suicide in 1984. Or that his mother, Dora, would also kill herself, throwing herself out a fourteenth-floor window in 1988.

But Carmen did not allow the death of Carlos to destroy her.

Over the years, she pursued the men who had killed him with the same determination with which she demanded that his body be returned to her for burial. For years and years, she was never deterred, not even when judge after judge dismissed her lawsuits, insisting on applying the amnesty before her accusations could even be investigated. But Pinochet's retirement from the army and his arrest in London opened the way for a change. In August of 1999, the Fifth Circuit of the Santiago Court of Appeals accepted Judge Juan Guzmán's indictment of the officers of the Caravan of Death on charges of murder and kidnapping. She finally saw placed under arrest those men who had flown into Calama in that Puma helicopter and forever changed her life. Arellano and Arredondo and Morén Brito and Fernández Larios. All of them awaiting judgment and retribution.

With the biggest fish still to come.

And so it came to pass that on April 27 of the year 2000, Carmen Hertz, representing her husband, argued in front of the Supreme Court that General Augusto Pinochet Ugarte was directly responsible for the executions and kidnappings carried out by Arellano's retinue and therefore should lose his senatorial immunity and face prosecution. The evidence she gave was overwhelming: testimonies by a string of officers in the zone who had protested the murder of unarmed and already sentenced prisoners and who had been shown the orders whereby General Pinochet named Arellano his personal delegate at a time of State of Siege and State of War, when no subordinate would have dared to act without the full agreement and knowledge of the Commander in Chief. Other documents attest to Pinochet's efforts to cover up the massacres, demanding—in orders scribbled in his very own handwriting, a real smoking gun!—that his subordinates erase any critical references to Arellano's mission in their reports. And she ended her statement by pointing to a conclusive indication of Pinochet's involvement and guilt: the systematic promotions given to the members of the Caravana de la Muerte and the automatic cashiering (and often persecution) of every officer who had shown the slightest resistance to their murderous spree, the slightest sign of humanity and decency.

So we were finding out, finally, how Carlos and the others had died. And we had found out when and where.

But the why was still there, hanging heavily in the air.

The answer was given, I believe, by Major Reveco—he who had been demoted, beaten and arrested because he had been too merciful towards the followers of Salvador Allende. In an interview with the English journalist Isabel Hilton for a BBC documentary, he suggested that the Caravan of Death had been meant to sent a message, not primarily to the civilians of Chile, but to its military, ensuring that every soldier understood that softness towards the fallen enemy would not be tolerated. The army itself needed to be terrorized. "It was a demonstration," Reveco said, "that Pinochet had absolute power." A sign, I might add, that the laws of the past that had marked our history were no longer valid, that there was no place for concord and reconciliation among Chileans. A sign that Pinochet was not going to be a mere interlude between democratic governments, that he intended to remake the face of Chile until it became unrecognizable.

So the death of Carlos Berger and the others cannot be understood as an accident, but rather as the cornerstone and foundation upon which General Pinochet was to build his fearful dominion in the seventeen years to come.

And there is something obstinately appropriate that it should be this death that may bring the General crashing down, that may open the door to his trial in the same land that he ruled so ferociously for so long. Germán Berger Hertz, no longer a little blonde dwarf, now almost as old as his father was the day he was assassinated, watched his mother stand there in court like an avenging angel, twenty-seven years after the military informed her that they had just killed her husband and would not return his body. Who could have dared to dream that she would be publicly accusing the most powerful man to ever rule that land of murder, demanding justice in the name of Carlos and all the dead of Chile?

• • • • •

Augusto Pinochet has just been deliciously trapped in the web of his own perversity. When our former dictator made thousands of political prisoners disappear into the night and fog of his dictatorship, leaving them without a burial, not even in his saddest nightmares could he have anticipated the joke that history was going to play on him: that many years later, it is those crimes that have allowed the Chilean Supreme Court, this eighth day of August 2000, to strip the General of his self-granted parliamentary immunity.

If only he had returned those bodies to their relatives instead of disappearing them, he would now be free.

Back then, when the first executions were carried out and the first denials were pronounced, refusing families the bodies of their murdered loved ones must have seemed a brilliant idea to Pinochet and his disciples. This was not accidental, a mere whim on the part of one or two sadists or a madman on the loose. It was systematic, deliberate, planned, meticulously and obstinately executed. This way, the military could have its cake and eat it too. It could kill its adversaries and not be held accountable for those killings, investing itself with the total power over life and death, yet simultaneously cleansing itself with an official dismissal of any guilt, insisting that there were no prisoners and that the disappearances were an invention of troublemakers. But we knew, everybody

Ariel Dorfman

in Chile was aware of what was really happening, happening interminably in nearby basements and remote deserts. Happening interminably: that is the sick logic of repression, the definition of a terror that will not stop.

When Pinochet condemned the relatives to the inferno of absolute uncertainty about the fate of the people they loved, he was forcing them and the rest of Chile to imagine, over and over again, those unnamable things that were being inflicted at that very moment on the men and women held captive. As there was no body to lay to rest, there could be no mental rest either. Torture was transformed from something merely physical into an event that was repeated incessantly in each citizen's inner world, paralyzing him or her with fear. Those disappearances ended up symbolizing for many of us the vanishing of the country itself, the attempt to destroy forever the Chile of liberty we had once inhabited. If the Caravan of Death was a message sent to the military to behave or else, the *desaparecidos* ended up being a message to the whole country: We are the lords not only of life but of death itself and we will punish not only you but damn those left behind to mourn you without surcease.

It is particularly marvelous, then, that it should be precisely those missing and supposedly dead bodies that have come back to haunt Pinochet, turning into the instrument of what might well be his punishment and that of his accomplices. To get off scot-free, Pinochet will now have to prove that he killed those prisoners. He would have to disinter every last one of them from the depths of their anonymous graves, drag them out of the rivers and the seas where they were cast, piece together the splinters of bone scattered over hills and fields. Then and only then would the offense cease to be ongoing and perpetual. Then and only then could the amnesty that Pinochet granted to himself be applied, according to Judge Guzmán's interpretation of the law: He would be freed because he had, admittedly, committed murder. Poetic justice indeed: It is the particular excesses of the General's own brand of extreme cruelty that have ended up ensnaring him.

It could not, of course, have been done without the unremitting struggle of the relatives of the missing who always refused to believe that their loved ones had died and who always proclaimed, against all odds, that justice was not impossible. And they have been almost alone in that steadfast belief for the last decade. I have described how, during our years of banishment, those of us in exile would fantasize about retribution, a heroic homecoming, a Chile regenerated by a rebellious populace, Pinochet judged under the majesty of the Andes. And though those reveries did not seem immediately attainable once we began trickling back home, I think that the core of the country clung to the conviction that some sort of justice would prevail. Paradoxically, it was only when democracy returned to our country that the possible trial of Pinochet began to appear even less feasible than before. Of course, the dictator had granted himself amnesty and had appointed himself to Congress as Senator for Life and had made sure no democratic president could change the command of the armed forces, making them the ultimate guarantors of his and their impunity.

Yes, but the greatest barrier was really created by many of the dictatorship's most resolute opponents who, once they took office, proved to be excessively prudent and misguidedly pragmatic. They feared, perhaps with good reason, that the slightest attempt to put the tyrant on trial would break the delicate equilibrium of the transition—and jeopardize their relations with the wealthy masters of Chile's economy. But this fear also became a pretext. In the name of "being realistic," the former dissidents settled into a pusillanimous consensus, implying that it was best to let the past slowly die, let yesterday's offenses against human rights slowly be forgotten. They prayed that Pinochet's eventual demise might resolve the issue for them.

And many of us who thought the General had to be judged so that Chile could reach real reconciliation ended up buying that consensus, acquiescing to it. I feel that I contributed, in my own way, to that moral debacle that accompanied the transition to democracy. From 1990 onward, I spent long periods in Santiago, though in due time I decided to live permanently in the United States. Whenever I visited, I would make a point of going to see the relatives of the *desparecidos*. I marched with them, listened to their stories, wrote plays and poems and articles in which their tragedy was explored. On *el*

Día de los Muertos, the Day of the Dead, I watched their pain at not having a grave to bring flowers to, a resting place on this earth, and even while I admired their fierce determination to seek justice in the same city and on the same streets walked by the men who had killed their loved ones, I remained morosely unable to imagine a different future, one where Pinochet would not be above the law and the missing could rest in peace. So I did what so many of my fellow Chileans do when confronted by a task that seems overwhelming and out of reach: I accepted that history was simply not on our side, I gave way to accommodation, my conscience endured and sanctified the inevitability of injustice, I grew accustomed to the General's malignancy in our midst. I had one advantage: As a writer, I could explore in my stories the dilemma of how you coexist with evil and what this does to trust and love, how it corrupts the national soul. But even as I bore witness from near and from afar, I never expected the situation to ever change. I grew tired of Pinochet, of pain, of impunity. Pinochet? Not Pinochet, not him again. Yes, like so many of my compatriots, I had lost my bearings.

And then the arrest and prosecution of our own criminal abroad erupted in the national conscience like a moral earthquake, shaming us into the trial that has just completed its first stage in our Supreme Court today. It is still too early to guess what the repercussions of this decision will be, whether Pinochet will manage to avoid an indictment by Judge Guzmán, whether further proceedings will be aborted due to medical reasons—which is probably the scenario the democratic government favors. Nor can we anticipate the sort of pressure the armed forces might exert in the months to come, along with the protests by Pinochet's powerful supporters.

Whatever happens to the General's transitory body, there can be no doubt that the Chilean Supreme Court's recent decision has implications for the rest of the planet, a lesson to be learned. The strategy of disappearing prisoners, that extreme form of violence that has sullied so many regimes of every ideology all over the world, has proven to be a boomerang that ends up damaging those who use it. The *desaparecidos*, it turns out, those men and women arrested one night and then never heard of again, have refused to accept the destiny of oblivion and terror that a dictator dreamt for them, are somehow still alive, beyond death, still accusing the man who thought he could extinguish them forever by hastening and then denying their deaths. Perhaps the past, after all, is not as easy to murder as some in power would like to proclaim. The hidden light of the men and women who gave their lives for what they believed in cannot be totally snuffed out, not while there is one person somewhere in this world who is willing to remember and resurrect them. That's all it takes, one person crying out in the ethical wilderness, one person and then one more and then another, that's all that's needed to keep the spark of justice alive.

That is the lesson that Pinochet's punishment ultimately offers us: At times it is right to dream the impossible, to ask for the impossible, to shout for the impossible.

History might happen to be listening. History just
might happen to answer.

$$\bullet \ \bullet \ \bullet \ \bullet \ \bullet$$

*I met Isabel Morel the same night I met the man who
was then her husband, Orlando Letelier. Exile was to
turn Isabel and her four sons into some of our best
friends. Indeed, it is strange to think that if it had not
been for Pinochet and his coup I would probably not
have had the chance and privilege to receive Isabel like
a long-lost sister into my life. And stranger still that the
night we first met was also to be the only time I would
ever spend with Orlando.*

*It was a Thursday, if I'm not mistaken—Thursday,
September the fifth, 1973. The day before, September
fourth, had been the third anniversary of Allende's victory in the presidential elections. Perhaps we knew we were
saying good-bye to our president—many of us in the
marching crowd of almost a million went by Allende's
balcony in La Moneda twice, as if we were hoping to
freeze this moment in time, daring it never to depart.*

*There was not much talking the next night when I
met Orlando. Fernando Flores, the Ministro Secretario
General de Gobierno, Allende's chief of staff—whose
cultural and media adviser in the last months of the*

Unidad Popular government I had been—had organized a thank-you and farewell party for General Carlos Prats, who had a few weeks before resigned his post as Commander in Chief of the Army. A far more terrible blow for our government than we even imagined at first. Not only because Prats had been the main support of the constitutional government, a man who had begun to define the security of Chile in terms that left Cold War ideology behind, proclaiming that a nation is secure when it has real sovereignty and its people are well fed, housed, healthy, free, educated, but also because his replacement was, of course, Pinochet.

At some point in the evening, dancing began. A tango was played. In my mind I see three couples circling, turning, becoming the music: First I see Orlando Letelier dancing with Sofía Prats, the wife of Carlos Prats; then into my field of vision comes Isabel dancing with José Tohá, who murmurs the words of the tango gently as they shuffle across the floor; and then I see Carlos Prats himself turning around and around with Tohá's wife, Moy.

All three had been ministers of defence for Allende, all three had been close to the military, all three were witnesses to the betrayal by the military of their vows, all three knew too much. All three would eventually be silenced.

They were so alive, the music was so vibrant—they glided along the wooden floors of the Peña de los Parra where we were holding our farewell dinner as if the tango could purify and postpone what was descending upon us. They hummed to each other the songs as if they could dance forever, as if they could hold the future at bay forever.

First Tohá was murdered and then Prats and Sofía in Buenos Aires and finally Orlando Letelier in Washington, D.C.

One might think that no act of Pinochet could have been more foolish, more arrogant and presumptuous, than this decision to kill one of Allende's former ministers in the capital of the United States, the country that had helped put the General in power and was doing all it could to keep him there.

Pinochet had already sent a message to the military and to the Chileans inside the country. Now it was our turn to hear him, those of us who had fled abroad. It was as if he were saying: There is no place safe on this planet for any of you. If you think that exile allows you freedom, you are wrong. You who escaped from me, you who danced that night, you will not dance again, you have no right to music or tangos or love. I am the god of silence. I own your bodies.

But in this, at least, he was wrong. General Pinochet knew a lot about death. But it is possible to say this and say it unequivocally: He knew and still knows so little about life.

He could kill Orlando, but he did not own his body.

We own the body of Orlando. Those of us who, in Chile and the United States, norteamericanos and

Ariel Dorfman

chilenos dancing together in a different way, helped to bring his murder to light, who tracked down his murderers, who made it possible for the first step towards justice be taken when Manuel Contreras, the head of Pinochet's secret police, was condemned to prison for ordering that assassination.

The owners of Orlando's body are those who survived him and did not allow a second implacable form of death to claim him, the death by forgetfulness and amnesia and distance. We could not stop the General's men from shattering the legs that had danced that night in Chile, we could not stop the General's men from destroying the lips that had sung the tango. We are not the lords of death to decide who lives and who dies.

But we are the ones who give meaning to that death, we are the guardians of that life and that memory even if Orlando and Sofía and José can no longer dance with us. And if I insist on this dancing metaphor it is because it also joins us to the cueca sola, the dance that the women of the disappeared have been dancing with their absent men. Our invisible dance with Orlando and all our missing loves has served the same function as the cueca sola: to make sure he is always present, to make sure that they are not killed again, refusing to let death have the last word.

If this were a fairy tale, here is how I would end it:

Once upon a time there was a country where three couples danced tango.

Once upon a time a man called Orlando Letelier was in our midst.

Once upon a time we needed help to keep him and so many others alive.

Once upon a time many people inside and outside Chile decided not to let my country die.

● ● ● ● ●

This is not, however, a fairy tale.

Isabel Morel Letelier has an interpretation of how Pinochet became the man we are now waiting to judge. Not an ogre beyond humanity, not the quintessential embodiment of evil. Just a man.

She first met him towards the end of August 1973. Isabel's friend Moy had already told her about Pinochet, describing him as a gallant, obliging, good-natured man, who used to ask the Tohá children to call him *Tata*. Pinochet had come up to Isabel in a reception held in honor of Orlando Letelier's having just been named as Allende's minister of defence and told her that he felt fortunate to be able to make her acquaintance. 'And what's also fortunate,' Pinochet added, 'is that every wife of every minister is so good-looking.' He had gone on like this, outdoing himself in courtesies, asking about her four sons, assuring her that the army was proud that Orlando—'our Orlando,' as Pinochet called him—was now a minister...'Because he is one of our boys,' he said, referring to Orlando's past as a military cadet and his excellent record of service before he had left the military academy.

"I had the impression," Isabel told me, "that here was a man who would go out of his way to please me. And this version of a honeyed and even groveling Pinochet was confirmed to me by Orlando, who was soon complaining about how servile and fawning this man was, to the point of making him nervous. 'He makes me uncomfortable,' Orlando explained. 'He wants to carry my briefcase, this from a General! And he tries to help me put my coat on. You know who he reminds me of? Those *hombrecitos*, those humble little men who used to assist the barber in old-time barbershops, who would come with a tiny broom to brush off the hairs from your jacket after your hair has been cut, and then they put out a hand and you have to give them a tip.' "

Three weeks later, Isabel saw Pinochet again. It was a few days after the coup. The wives of Allende's ministers who had been arrested know nothing about the whereabouts of their husbands, so Isabel and her friend Moy de Tohá go to ask for a meeting with Pinochet to the Ministry of Defence where he was then installed. As they went up the stairs from one floor to the next, they were frisked, supposedly for security reasons, over and over in a way that Isabel described as extremely crude, but whose real purpose, she thought, was to humiliate them. By coincidence, they run into Pinochet, surrounded by a flock of photographers, who is advancing down a corridor. He embraces and kisses Moy, as if she were still his old friend and not the wife of the man he has taken prisoner. Moy cannot know, that first time she sees Pinochet after the coup and feels his lips on her cheek, that five months later she will be standing in front of him one more time, begging for her husband's life. For now, she is relieved that Pinochet will receive them. He orders a nearby colonel to set up a "meeting for these ladies."

They are asked to come back in a few days' time, on September 23—Isabel remembers the exact date because that is the day of Pablo Neruda's funeral. They miss the massive burial of Chile's greatest poet, which turned into the first public outpouring of grief and defiance against the dictatorship, those chants and shouts of the mourners a harbinger of the resistance that was to keep on growing in the years ahead. Instead, Isabel and Moy and Irma, the wife of former minister of foreign affairs Clodomiro Almeyda, wait for a long time, sitting on two sofas in a large reception room in the Ministry of Defence.

"All of a sudden," Isabel told me, "behind me I hear the door open and a series of incoherent shouts begin to come through it, a nervous voice saying, 'Their husbands are in perfect condition, well nourished, well dressed, they are doing fine.' I turn around and there is Pinochet coming into the room, incredibly angry. At the very moment that I turned to look at him he was screaming, 'If things had been the other way around, then. . .' And Pinochet passed his index finger across his throat and stuck out his tongue grotesquely, making a grimace, as if he had been strangled or his throat had been slit. And I had to contain myself, not to laugh. Maybe because I had spent so many years abroad, when Orlando was in the Interamerican Bank and then as ambassador to Washington, but I just had developed this sense of humor and it seemed, well, so absurd. There we were, three defenseless women who had been checked by all these security guards, with our husbands disappeared, and he was the one who was scared, he was the one who was angry. At us. *Alteradísimo.*"

I interrupted Isabel. "This sounds just like the temper tantrum he had with Moy five months later, when she went to see him again."

"It seems that after the coup Pinochet was angry all the time," Isabel answered. "Because then he began screaming even louder, referring to Allende: 'And that traitor, even if he's underground...' And then Irma stood up and said: 'That language is unacceptable, General,' and she began to leave the room. And that seemed to calm Pinochet down a bit, he sobered up. 'What brings you here, ladies?' "

Each wife explained what was worrying her, Isabel saying that she was receiving calls from the States, from Holland, from other places around the world, wanting to know where Orlando was, and she didn't know what to say. She had had no news from her husband. None of them did.

"Regarding this," Pinochet said, "there can be no response." And reiterated that the men were being given clothing, food, were in perfect condition. Again, very angry.

"Please let us contact our husbands."

"Impossible."

"But the children," Moy said. "Carolina and José. They want to find out about their father. You know them."

Pinochet hesitated for a second and then: "All right, they can write a letter to him."

"And how about us?"

"All right, you as well, you as well, write, write something."

Isabel said that all three of the women present felt heartened by this development: If letters could be written it meant that their husbands were alive. But Moy did not think this was enough: "And what about the other wives?" she asked, because there were so many others who needed to send a message to their loved ones.

"All right, do it, do it, do it. They can also write something." Pinochet's voice full of exasperation, as if he had been forced to honor some strange military code of battlefield justice which says that if one person is given a privilege everybody else should have the same chance.

And that was the last time Isabel Morel de Letelier ever saw General Augusto Pinochet Ugarte.

Haunted by the question that I have also been asking myself so obsessively: How to understand the abyss between one Pinochet and the other, how had the gallant and bootlicking man of three weeks before turned into this gargoyle?

I asked her.

"Look," she said, "Pinochet realizes a few days before the coup that everyone is conspiring and he does not want to join, he simply does not want to join, but at some point he says to himself, 'If I don't get involved in this, they're going to kill me.' And that's why—because he joins the coup very late in the game—he takes on that vulgar language, that boastfulness, so nobody will think he is docile. He has to mount the others as if they were horses, he's got to be always angry, he's got to instill fear in everybody."

"Why?"

"*Porque tiene un miedo pánico.* Because he's scared out of his wits. That's how you understand Pinochet. He's a survivor."

Can this reading of Pinochet be true?

For so long I have been trying to figure out how we should exorcise Pinochet and all this time, without our even realizing it, maybe he was the one trying desperately to exorcise us from his life, like Macbeth trying to sleep, trying to rid himself of his ghosts.

Could this be the secret that unlocks the enigma of Pinochet? Could it be that simple? That the only way for Pinochet himself to erase the man who carried Orlando Letelier's briefcase was to kill Orlando Letelier? That the only way to forget the man who had sworn friendship and loyalty to Carlos Prats was to order the assassination of Carlos Prats? That the only way to deny the man who had taken gifts to the children of José Tohá was to murder their father? That all this time the person he was most scared of was none other than himself, the man he had once been, the man he had effectively suffocated to death when he joined the conspiracy against Allende?

Qué grandísimo hijo de puta.

What a son of a bitch.

And to think that I had almost fallen into the trap of feeling sorry for him.

· · · · ·

I am in Porto Alegre, Brazil, this last week of January 2001, attending the first meeting of the World Social Forum, the counter-globalization movement's answer to the gathering in Davos, Switzerland, of the world's most powerful political and economic leaders (where I had myself been an eccentric guest, as a Forum Fellow, in February of 1998). The theme and slogan of our gathering here in Porto Alegre—twenty thousand participants from almost as many grassroots organizations from around the world crisscrossing each other like bees in search of a hive in the hot, humid weather of Brazil—is "Another World Is Possible," the certainty that the members of the planet's ruling elite are wrong when they proclaim the dogma that there is no viable alternative to the current dominant form of global capitalism. Though my primary interest in coming here has been to learn from so many experiences—and to explore how the artistic imagination and models of critical inquiry can contribute to this vast multitude of movements—I find myself instead constantly besieged by another sort of question, over and over again, the same insatiable query from all quarters: What will happen with Pinochet?

One would have thought that by now, five months after the Supreme Court stripped Pinochet of his immunity, there would be no need to ask me this. Hasn't he been arraigned yet? In fact, no. He has not even been formally charged. Well, yes, he was formally charged on December 1, 2000 by Judge Juan Guzmán, but that accusation was found to be technically flawed by an appellate court which threw it out on the grounds that the defendant first had to be granted a deposition and the Supreme Court has since ruled twice on that verdict originally favorable to the General, overturning it once and then a week later clarifying that ruling and partly reversing it, mandating medical exams as well as an interrogation.

It is all very intricate and tiresome and protracted—and perhaps this is what Pinochet's lawyers are looking for, to delay by any means possible the moment when he is officially branded by the investigating judge as a murderer and kidnapper and placed under arrest, fingerprinted, his photo taken for mug shots, the start of the trial itself. Every hour that passes, every appeal that must be heard, every technicality that is invoked, allows time to pass and it is time that is the General's main ally, time that corrodes his already frail body that houses a mind that may or may not be weakening. Constant postponement in the hope that when Pinochet is finally examined to determine if he is healthy enough to stand trial, the defendant will be found absolutely unfit. It is a replay of the whole England caper, but this time with even more lawyers disputing every decision. Who will conduct the tests? Will he be examined in the intimidating atmosphere of the Hospital Militar? Is there a guarantee that the pathological tests will not be doctored? Will the tests be made public? What if he doesn't show up for the medical tests? What if he doesn't respond to the summons? The drama of the give and take has been somewhat relieved by the comic effect of watching Pinochet caught in the bind of the exams themselves. He desperately needs to be found in utter disrepair but Chilean law—in an arcane definition that goes back to the nineteenth century—declares that the only causes for a defendant to be dismissed from standing trial are if he is insane or dementedly senile, categories that the former dictator wishes just as desperately to avoid. Mindful of the way he will be remembered by future generations, the General would do anything—well, almost anything—not to go down in history as crazy or an imbecile.

The outcome may come down to a matter of semantics. A few weeks ago, I got a call from Luis Fornazzari, a Chilean-born neurologist and psychiatrist at the University of Toronto, reputedly one of the world's pre-eminent specialists in senile dementia—who has just accepted an offer to fly from Canada to Chile to be one of the eight-member medical team examining Pinochet. He found himself in an uncomfortable position: having to conduct tests on the man who had exiled him and killed many of his friends and, at the same time, be scientifi-

Ariel Dorfman

cally objective about the state of Pinochet's mind. "If he's mentally incapacitated," he told me, "I will most definitely deem him unfit to stand trial." What worried him was that the other doctors and psychologists might be more open to pressures from the government, armed forces and others, to exaggerate the General's ailments just a little bit, just enough to get the old man off the hook, and he did not want to be a party to condoning any such political maneuver.

At first, it seemed that Dr. Fornazzari's worries were misplaced. After several days of procrastination by Pinochet, who simply did not show up for his exams, a reluctant General was convinced by Izurieta, the present Commander in Chief of the Army, that he absolutely needed to obey the law and that the military was in no position to oppose this or any other court order. During four mornings and four afternoons, January 10 through 13, Pinochet submitted to a barrage of tests, with the result that he was diagnosed as suffering a "slight to moderate subcortical vascular dementia" that would not impede his standing trial. And so, having helped to write the final medical report, Dr. Fornazzari headed back to Toronto—only to discover that the official report issued the following week had doctored the results, eliminating the word "slight" and changing the diagnosis to "severely moderate," a change that, along with other alterations, would have made it easier for Judge Guzmán to dismiss the charges against a man who could not, according to one interpretation of that report, defend himself.

A scandal erupted. Dr. Fornazzari refused to sign the doctored report and sent his own conclusions directly to Guzmán and though his determination—in which he resolutely confirmed the original diagnosis—was attacked by the minister of justice as "irresponsible" and by right-wing newspapers as "biased," it at least offered the investigating judge the leeway to finally conduct a preliminary oral deposition of Pinochet on January 23 at which the General—surprise, surprise—denied ever having ordained anybody's murder or kidnapping. Whether that meaningful event—the first time in his life the former dictator had been forced to answer questions about his misdeeds—will have any bearing on the case is anybody's guess.

That, at any rate, is where things stood at the moment when I left the States for Brazil, and it was as much as I could explain to my anxious questioners at the World Social Forum. Would Guzmán bow to pressure and terminate the trial ahead of time, adducing the "severely moderate" senility with which the defendant had been (falsely) diagnosed? Or would he decide, based upon his own two-hour questioning of Pinochet, that the accused has only a "mild" case of senescence?

Semantics. The battle for meaning and nuance.

But there is nothing mild or nuanced or ambiguous about Guzmán's decision once it reaches us here on January 29 just the day before the forum in Porto Alegre is about to close.

The Chilean judge, almost a year after Pinochet

returned home from England and seemed to have, literally, gotten away with murder, officially charges him. He notifies the former dictator, former senator, former head of state, former strongman, Augusto José Ramón Pinochet Ugarte, that he is being put on trial (*sometido a proceso*) as the *author* of the crimes of kidnapping and homicide of the persons of Claudio Arturo Lavín Loyola, Pablo Renán Vera Torres, Eugenio Ruiz Tagle Orrego—and fifty-four other names; and also for the kidnapping of Miguel Enrique Muñoz Flores and Carlos Berger Guralnik and Harold Ruperto Cabrera Abarzúa and fifteen other names, in all seventy-three victims of the Caravan of Death. The document also specifies, I am told from Chile, that the accused is to be placed under house arrest (*prisión preventiva*), in his own home, calle Pedro Lira Urquieta #11.280, in La Dehesa (Santiago), to be kept in custody suitable to an army officer. And that the judge has furthermore decreed that at some point soon the General will be fingerprinted, photographed and submitted to the usual police procedures that accompany such indictments.

Though I am tempted to fly across the South American continent to hug my friends of the Association of Relatives of the Disappeared—who are now free to roam every inch of Chile while their nemesis is confined, guarded, disgraced—I can, in fact, think of no better place to celebrate this victory than Porto Alegre. Most of those present at the World Social Forum have journeyed here from countries where they have to face on a daily basis an array of local would-be Pinochets. The work they try to do, demanding health care for all and credit for the poorest sectors of society and transparency in the corporations that rule their world and accountability from the government bureaucracies that supposedly oversee those corporations, the work that these activists do in the alternative media and the struggle for ecological survival, for the rights of indigenous people and against discrimination and child labor, all this and so much more inevitably pits them against the most powerful members of their societies and therefore entails the risk of clashes, day in and day out, with the security forces. For most of the NGO militants here in Porto Alegre, the symbolic punishment of someone like Pinochet somewhat ties the hands of the men in their own countries who are ready to kill and torture in the name of stability and order, sends them a message, facilitates democracy. It is to people like the ones who surround me, those who resist in the Philippines and China and India and Guatemala and Ecuador and Kenya, that the Pinochet verdict and imprisonment matters. It protects and emboldens them.

It is here in Porto Alegre—standing on a platform with the Madres de la Plaza de Mayo, speaking of the *desaparecidos* as a metaphor for all the neglected, forgotten people of the world who live and die as if they had never existed—that I measure the truly global nature of our triumph in Chile.

Pinochet is not above the law.

Ariel Dorfman

He does not quite realize it yet.

But he will, he will. He will know it on that day I have imagined so often that I can conjure the scene up as if I were in the room: A large, muscular man will take in his own thick hands one of those hands of Pinochet that I have been thinking of for so long, he will start to slowly blot those fingers of Pinochet with black ink and then, very slowly and deliberately, so as not to stain the General's clothes or tie, he will secure the fingerprints, a thumb and now the index and now the next finger as well, one by one by one. And from that moment onward that page with the impression of those ten fingers will form part of the criminal record.

That moment, yes. *El momento de la realidad*, we would say in Spanish. The moment when reality dawns upon him, inescapably traps him in its mirror.

That unveiled moment I have been dreaming of for years.

The moment after they have finished taking his fingerprints, that next moment when it will at last be time to take a mug shot of Citizen Augusto Pinochet Ugarte.

First one side of the face, then the other side, and finally the last shot looking straight at the camera, straight at us who can see him, perhaps we can start to really see him for the first time.

That's it, *mi General*. That's right.

As if you were a criminal.

Como si fuera un criminal.

• • • • •

It must have been sometime in 1974—the middle? late in the year?—I can only be sure of the year and that it must have happened in France, that's when I think I first lay eyes on María Josefa Ruiz Tagle. She was a baby girl—around a year and a half old, I guess, and if I'm not mistaken she played on the floor of our kitchen in Paris with our son Rodrigo, who was then seven years old, while we chatted with her mother, Mónica Espinoza. Angélica says I am mistaken, that I could not have seen María Josefa then because Mónica had come to Europe at that point without her child—and yet that memory burns within me still, I can remember oh so clearly being charmed by the beauty of the baby but even more by the serenity of the mother.

I had known Mónica's husband, Eugenio Ruiz Tagle Orrego, only vaguely, just a hello and good-bye a couple of times in the halls of our party's headquarters (we both belonged to the same revolutionary organization). Mutual friends keep on telling me that we must have met and talked any number of times, but I can't for the life of me recall much else, other than trying to squeeze from the memory bag in my head one or two occasions in which we exchanged a joke or two; that's all I remember of his life. His death, however, was another matter. A civil engineer who came from one of Chile's most aristocratic families and a dedicated revolutionary since his student days at the Catholic University, the coup had found him in Antofogasta, in the north of the country, acting as general manager of the National Cement Works. He had voluntarily given himself up on September 12, like so many who had trusted that the military would not defile or denigrate them—and had been killed a month or so later, reportedly in the most savage fashion.

A disturbing rumor had sprung up after his death: that his right-wing father in Santiago had taken his time in pressuring the military to release the wayward offspring, apparently because he thought that nothing much could happen to the young man, given the traditional civility of Chile's armed forces, or maybe trusting that his son's blue-blooded heritage would protect him. Which made it even more heartbreaking when his mother demanded that Eugenio's tightly sealed coffin be opened and discovered his body and face mutilated almost beyond recognition. But I always wondered if those reports of his father's guilty detachment and subsequent intolerable loss did not constitute a fabrication of the sort that often circulate in uncertain and violent times, an attempt by a repressed community to forge a story of how the murder of a rebellious son awakens a conservative progenitor to the true evil of a regime he helped to bring into being.

What was no fabrication, however, was how that death had devastated the family and you could see it in the deep well of sorrow that Mónica seemed to be floating in when we met her in Paris almost a year after the *execution of her husband. And yet, at the same time, there was an unexpected purity in her gaze as I recall it, as if she had decided not to give fate the satisfaction of seeing her cry, as if all the tears had dried up inside her instead of coming out. Or was it a quiet resilience?— a decision she seemed to have made that she was going to get on with life, no matter how hard that might be, for the sake of the baby, but also in the name of her dead love, who would not have wanted the murder of his body to have also murdered her future. So I was not entirely surprised when I heard, some months later, that she had settled into a stable relationship with José Joaquín Brunner, a friend of hers and Eugenio's from way back. Brunner, whom I was also close to, was at the time working on his doctorate at Oxford and would become, upon his return to Chile a few years later with Mónica and María Josefa, one of the country's most prominent intellectuals.[4] But perhaps more essential to Mónica, José Joaquín grew into the role of María Josefa's daddy, bringing her up as if she were his own child.*

The little girl was told from an early age that her biological father, Eugenio, had died in front of a firing squad, but no other details were forthcoming. She conjured up, María Josefa wrote many years later, a sort of romantic scene—a death occasioned by a diffuse group of men, none of whom was identifiably responsible, perhaps a way of keeping that violence done to her father from overwhelming and poisoning her life, by not making her wonder about who was personally responsible for that

Ariel Dorfman

homicide. She always sensed, nevertheless, that under- neath the silence surrounding and covering that remote death, there lurked something more dreadful, some secret terror that was all the more fearful because nobody dared to name it. And then, one day, when she was twelve, a strange hunch led her to probe and explore what might lie behind a photograph in her grandmother's house, a picture which showed María Josefa herself at around two years of age taking a bath in a small tub. Was it the clean water in which she was bathing in the picture that provoked her to undo the frame that held it and go beyond the false innocence of that child she had once been? Perhaps, because what she found were three pages hidden by her grandmother and written by two of her father's friends who had witnessed the way he had been treated before he died, witnesses who had been tortured themselves but who had, by a miracle, survived instead of being killed by the Caravan of Death. Reading those words from the past, María Josefa found out that Eugenio had not been shot by a firing squad, but—to use her own words—"he was missing an eye. They had carved out his nose. His face was deeply burnt in many places. His neck had been broken. Stabs and bullet wounds. The bones broken in a thousand parts. They had torn the nails from his hands and from his feet. And they had told him that they were going to kill me and my mother."

But she said nothing. She kept those words, those images, inside. Like the country itself.

Many years later, in 1999, when she had Lucas, her

first baby—at the age of twenty-six, the age her father had reached upon his death—when she held the baby in her arms and realized that her father had also been able to hold her and get to know her, she burst into tears one morning and felt the irresistible need to write to her father, to tell her story, what it meant to be the child not only of a murdered man but of a country that did not want to confront and name that death. She denounced how everything around her had been built so she and everyone else would not have to look the past in the face. Built, she said, so that people would never have to go to sleep every night feeling afraid.

Still, however, she kept those intimate words to herself. Until, a year and a half later, in November 2000, when Eugenio's body was exhumed from the Antofagasta cemetery and taken to the Wall of Memory in Santiago for a second burial. Then she allowed an actor to publicly read out, on that occasion, the words she had written to her father. For the tears that had been kept hidden all these years to come out, the tears I had not been able to see when we sat with her mother Mónica in that kitchen in Paris and I watched the fatherless child playing, for that to happen, first Pinochet had to be stripped of his immunity and Eugenio's name had to be cleared—he was not a terrorist but a victim, he was not a criminal but a hero, and his death was terrible but had not been entirely in vain as it had come back to haunt the man who had ordered it. First Eugenio had to come back from the dead. Then his daughter could come out into the light of day.

Ariel Dorfman

But that is not the end of the story. When you drag something out from its hiding place, other things emerge, one thing leading to another. Eugenio Ruiz Tagle still had one more service to perform for his family and his friends and his country.

When Judge Guzmán placed General Pinochet under house arrest at the end of January 2001, his lawyers immediately appealed—insisting that their client was innocent, that there was no proof that he had known about any of the deaths of the Caravan of Death. One week later, on February 7, the online newspaper El Mostrador (these sorts of journals are the only really free sites in Chilean print media) published the most damning document yet in the whole case. Back in 1973 Pinochet's justice minister—probably because of Ruiz Tagle's family connections—had informed the Commander in Chief of the Army of the young man's torture and extrajudicial execution by the officers from the Caravan of Death. In his own handwriting, Pinochet answered the minister that he was to deny the facts and conceal them, instructing him to say that "Mr. Ruiz Tagle was executed due to the grave charges that existed against him. [Say that] there was no torture according to our information." Needless to say, any possible investigation into that death had been quashed.

This piece of news occasioned yet another revelation the next day in the same online newspaper. Carlos Bau, an accountant at the Cement Works where Eugenio had been general manager and who had given himself up to *the authorities that same September 12, told the story of Ruiz Tagle's daily torture at the Air Force Base of Cerro Moreno in Antofagasta during the month that preceded his execution. The soldiers had wanted the prisoners to confess that they had weapons and explosives (Pinochet's subordinates were trying to assemble a justification for the repression their Commander in Chief had unleashed, proof that there was a war and that the enemy was armed and dangerous). It turned out that, far from protecting him, Ruiz Tagle's surnames had made his tormentors pick him out for special treatment—maybe to teach him a lesson, maybe because they had class resentments of their own, maybe because a Ruiz Tagle should have known better than to associate with the Allendista riffraff. Whatever the reasons, he was always the first to be beaten every time there was a session, constantly mocked and kicked and cut—and, like his wife a year later in Paris, like his daughter through most of her life, Eugenio had not let a cry out, had kept what he was feeling inside. But Bau added one more detail that had not up until that moment been public knowledge in Chile: the identity of the officer who had started the beating, who had begun it all by landing Eugenio a kick in the genitals as an introduction to what was to await him in the days ahead. It was Lieutenant Hernán Gabrielli Rojas. Who happened to be the present acting Commander in Chief of the Chilean Air Force. The same man.*

Are you sure? the journalist asked Bau.

Absolutely sure.

Ariel Dorfman

And in the next days, Bau's identification was confirmed by several other witnesses, Hernán Vera and Juan Ruz and another victim, an officer called Navarro, who added that he had also seen Gabrielli torturing a fourteen-year-old boy.

General Gabrielli's response on February 12 was not only to proclaim his innocence but also to announce that he was suing Bau and the others for libel—invoking a clause in the Law of National Security which shields a Commander in Chief from slander. The charges were subsequently dismissed ("We weren't slandering him," Bau said, "we were just telling the truth about him") and, later in the year, in spite of ferocious resistance from the air force, Gabrielli was forced to step down from his post.

Another side effect of the trial of General Pinochet. And another lesson to be learned.

Because terror is not conquered in one revelatory flash. It is a slow, zigzag process, just like memory itself. Let me make myself clearer: I had read the name Gabrielli as the tormentor of Ruiz Tagle back in 1976 or 1977, when Carlos Bau arrived in Holland (where our family had just moved from Paris). He had already served three years of a forty-year prison sentence which had been commuted into twenty years of banishment. Carlos had no qualms in recounting his terrifying story— though what I recalled above all of that conversation afterward was an image that surged into my head and stayed with me through the years, my realization that *when somebody has been tortured it is as if for the rest of their life they will be wearing sunglasses behind their eyes. A few days after Carlos arrived in Amsterdam, he journeyed to Geneva to offer his testimony to the Human Rights Commission and that's how, some time later, I was able to read it at my leisure, that's when I read, I must have read, the name of Gabrielli. Except that it completely slipped my mind. Not that peculiar. So many names and things and circumstances that we forget. No, what is special, what is painfully revealing, is that even though Carlos and the others had mentioned Gabrielli whenever they spoke about their experience, everybody else in Chile also forgot that name. Or simply did not pay attention. Or did not dare to pay attention. Or did not want to face the consequences of paying attention.*

Until the moment was right.

Until Pinochet's arrest and arraignment, his submission to the law like any mortal, broke his aura of invulnerability, shattering the dread with which he had frozen our hearts.

If María Josefa was finally able to speak and if the rest of us were able to finally hear what Carlos Bau had been telling us over and over for years, it was because they were no longer alone, it was because so many others near and faraway slowly began to open up. I am not making this up: Over and over I meet, on each visit to Chile, people who used to keep their eyes on the ground or shift them around while speaking of the years of terror, and now lift those eyes and meet my own gaze. I

Ariel Dorfman

could tell, for instance, the story of Felipe Agüero, the twin brother of my former brother-in-law Nacho (yes, the one who watched Pinochet's glove wave at us that evening in 1983), who recently, after seeing how Carlos Bau and his fellow detainees had brought down an Air Force general who had engaged in torture twenty-seven years ago, decided to finger one of his academic colleagues at the Catholic University as an interrogator in the infamous Estadio Nacional in Santiago, a certain political science professor called Emilio Meneses. I could retell his story and many others.

Better to end with this one: When I was working against Pinochet in the plebiscite of 1988, I met an old, toothless woman in a shantytown not far from our house in La Reina who had told me that she had dared not vote against Pinochet "because his eye sees everything, especially in the polling booth."

I ran into her again twelve years later, a few months after the General had been placed under house arrest in Santiago. This time she told me several jokes about the old man.

She no longer cared if Pinochet was secretly listening to her.

• • • • •

Today, July 9, 2001, by a vote of two to one a Chilean court of appeals temporarily suspended the trial of General Pinochet due to his mental incapacitation. And in this case, there are no more legal possibilities of an appeal—even though the lawyers for the victims have stated that they will attempt to do so. No, there is no way of reversing the decision of the judges.

The mind of Pinochet. The mind of Pinochet.

I can't get in there, into that mind, still can't really figure it out no matter how much I have tried since I first heard him speak to me over that phone in La Moneda all those years ago—and now it is that unfathomable mind of his that has saved him yet one more time, it has hidden him from us one more final, last, definitive time.

Here we have a man who just a few months ago—just before he underwent the medical exams that have freed him—was able to recognize, one by one, name by name, one hundred and twenty generals who visited him at his home to show support. Here is a man who was able to banter, in January, when he greeted Dr. Luis Fornazzari the first day of that medical exam, about Fornazzari's hometown of Iquique and mutual acquaintances that they both knew there. Here is a man who, the next day, observed that Dr. Fornazzari had a certain physical resemblance to Joan Garcés—the Spanish adviser to Allende who has hounded him—and when asked to elaborate a bit more on the comparison, suggested that it was not merely a matter of appearance and demeanor, but also because they were both part of the "accusing side" and then added, sardonically, "You're such a neurologist and such a psychiatrist, you can contact me later if you want more explanations." Playing games, Pinochet. Here is the man who, in England, just before being released, was told by a right-wing supporter, that when he returned to Chile it would be prudent that he no longer attend meetings of the Senate, given his deteriorated health, here is the man who answered: "Yes, but what if I get better when I return?" Here is the man who Dr. Fornazzari—who is an international expert working for the last twenty years with the International Working Group on Dementia and who can therefore quote experiments and results from Japan and Texas and Chicago and Helsinki and Ontario—has diagnosed as being perfectly able to stand trial, his disability being of a subcortical nature that does not impair the capacity to remember, discern, coordinate thoughts. But the majority of the Court of Appeals has nevertheless deemed in its wisdom that the General would be unable to answer questions or identify as his own the handwriting on a document where he asks a regional commander to lie about the Caravan of Death.

To reach that conclusion the judges have had to twist the law and reinterpret what dementia means, in a ruling that has so stretched the latitude of that concept that hundreds of prisoners who have been condemned and are serving jail sentences and have a worse mental condition than Pinochet's could now ask that their cases be reopened and that they be freed. The court has added the caveat that in the hypothetical case that Pinochet's mental condition experiences a remarkable recovery, the charges would be reinstated but everyone knows that this is a mere fiction. The General has been set free, to dodder off into his old age without ever having to answer another question about his crimes, because of political reasons.

The two judges who found him too sick to stand trial are conservatives. The doctors who deemed Pinochet to be unable to undergo the stress of the proceedings are not, like Dr. Fornazzari, living in Canada, but in a Chile where members of Pinochet's death squads are still on the loose, listening in to conversations and sending out threats. Those doctors and judges live in a country where the democratic government, though affecting a supposedly neutral stance, has been hoping all along that Pinochet's trial will not be held—because it will create tremendous and almost insurmountable tensions with the army. They live in a country where—is it very different anywhere else on this earth?—if you are rich and well connected you get a better chance at escaping justice than if you are poor and defenseless.

Here's the bottom line: From the very start, from the very moment the General was arrested by Scotland Yard, too many people with far too much power had an enormous stake in freeing Pinochet. What is amazing is that we have managed so many victories in this struggle of almost three years, that the General has only been able to avoid the dream I had for him by being proclaimed a dribbling idiot. Indeed, given that Pinochet was for twenty-five years the revered and undisputed leader of an army that did not lose its war and still holds a monopoly of firepower, it seems even more miraculous that it took the Pinochetistas almost a year and half to find a way to disgracefully squiggle their hero out of standing trial.

Is that why I feel strangely optimistic when I hear the news? Because I never expected the dictator, after all, to ever spend even one night under arrest? No, it is something deeper which fuels my sense of accomplishment, my need to celebrate this ending, even if it is not as perfect as I would have wanted it originally. During these months of tracking the General and watching him being hunted down, I have slowly come to the conviction that what happens to Pinochet's contingent and uncertain body is ultimately not as important as what this never-ending trial has already changed in the vast mind of humanity.

That mind of humanity is not something mystical, a mere utopian illusion, but a battleground of ideas and emotions in constant dispute. What constitutes us as a species is the stuttering and precarious attempt through the ages to determine what it means to be human and what rights we hold due to the defining circumstance of having been born. How to insure that those who systematically violate those rights cannot avoid their final and personal responsibility, their day of reckoning?

The Pinochet case will remain as a fundamental step in this search for a better humanity. And it will have clear practical effects: There are in the world today thousands of vile men who have destroyed the lives of their fellow citizens, who have raped and tortured their bodies, and who will in the future, solely because of the Pinochet extradition trial, not be able to travel abroad as they so cheerfully did in the past. These felons are, from now on, imprisoned within the borders of their own country.

During the century which is opening, they will never again sleep well at night. Now it's their turn to feel fear.

This is General Pinochet's irrefutable gift to humanity.

Thank you, General.

Now it's your turn to feel fear.

• • • • •

Or am I merely consoling myself with words that try to stir and inspire because tomorrow morning, for the first time in almost three years, General Pinochet will rise knowing that the only questions he will have to face are the questions the punishing mirror asks him, and never again another question from one of his victims?

THE SHADOW OF CHILE

SO, DID WE PASS the test the world sent us when Pinochet was returned to Chile? Did we purge the past we inherited from him that day in the National Stadium as we watched the women of the disappeared dancing by themselves, asking us to dance with them, have we not accomplished that task far too often forgotten or postponed amidst the morass of the transition? Hasn't the country that has emerged after the arrest and during the many trials of General Pinochet, hasn't that country been changed forever and for the better, hasn't this book insistently demonstrated that we succeeded beyond my wildest dreams?

That we did not entirely manage to finish the business begun in London and Madrid, the sad reality that we did not have the strength to morally transform our country enough to bring about that very special day when our former dictator would have been forced to hear the verdict of "guilty" in a court of law, this should serve as a warning, because it bespeaks an incomplete democracy, a land that has not yet entirely shaken off the traumatic aftereffects of brutality and terror. I do not doubt, however, that this deeper democratization of Chile will slowly dawn and I tell myself, living as I do abroad, not immersed in the day-to-day difficult struggle back home, that one must be patient.

Perhaps the day will come soon when we will be able to finally take back the country Pinochet stole from us, the country we allowed him to steal.

THE LONG GOOD-BYE TO TYRANTS

I OFTEN WONDER WHAT went through Slobodan Milosevic's mind in October of 1998 when he heard the news, perhaps at about the same time I was being shocked by it in California, that Augusto Pinochet had been arrested in London by detectives of Scotland Yard. Did Milosevic—at that point quite firmly the president of Yugoslavia—tremble at the idea that a foreign court could put former heads of state on trial in the name of the very humanity that those rulers had violated? Did he foresee in the Chilean General's fate what might befall him? Could he suspect that less than four years later he would be facing the International Criminal Court in The Hague?

As I made the rounds of radio and TV programs defending the need to put former dictators on trial in countries other than their own if those lands were incapable of doing so, I was invariably greeted by the misgivings of commentators and call-in listeners alike who were certain that indictments like the one Pinochet was facing would encourage oppressors to stay in power against all odds and settle into their bunkers until their last round of ammunition was spent. Wasn't it better to let the dictators go quietly with their spoils into the night of retirement and relieve the people suffering under their boot from the distress of a protracted civil conflict? Wasn't that a small price to pay for the lives saved? And wasn't this an affair best left to the citizens of the affected nation to decide?

Of all the arguments against the Pinochet trial, this seemed to me then and still seems to me now to be the most dangerous and the most specious. It presumes that tyrants leave when they feel like it and not when they are thrown out. In other words, it postulates that the people themselves are not the protagonists of their own history, the true and often secret architects of democracy. In the Chilean case, for instance, Pinochet tried to ignore the results of the 1988 plebiscite until the rest of the armed forces and the international community declared that they recognized the victory of the democratic forces. Don Augusto's weakness and isolation were the outgrowth of a vast mobilization of the Chilean people that cost us thousands of lives and hundreds of thousands of exiles and torture sessions and expulsions and beatings and persecutions—just as the struggle for liberty in Poland and Nigeria, in Indonesia and Haiti, South Africa and Czechoslovakia, was decisive in the collapse of the authoritarian regimes in those countries.

Tyrants don't leave because they are good. They leave because they have no other alternative, because they lost the battle for the imagination of the future, because millions of their compatriots were able to dream, deep in the private walls of their hearts and out there on the riskier streets of their city, another sort of world, a world where impunity does not and should not eternally reign.

My impassioned hymn to the power of ordinary citizens fell on deaf ears. Look at Milosevic, I was told. Wait and see, I was told: The trial of General Pinochet will delay the end of Milosevic indefinitely. Wait and see.

We waited and then we saw. We saw the people of Serbia rise against Milosevic in October 2000, barely two years after Pinochet's detention in London. We saw no pampering of the Yugoslav despot, no safeguards offered against future prosecutions in order to convince him to leave office. We saw that the predicted bloodbath did not materialize, despite the fact that no guarantee of total immunity was offered to Milosevic and his cronies, their position and popularity undermined, it is true, by the NATO bombing campaign. And it took less than a year for the former strongman of Serbia to be extradited to The Hague, where he is now trying to defend himself against charges of genocide at the United Nations tribunal. What I had hoped would happen to General Pinochet—his victims confronting him—has become the fate of Milosevic.

Such a scenario is not, of course, possible, without intense pressure from abroad (which, in the case of Milosevic, was made even more conspicuous by the U.S. threat to withhold a billion-dollar loan—a coercion that was not, of course, ever applied to Chile; the U.S. never demanded that Pinochet be extradited for the terrorist bomb that killed Letelier less than twenty blocks from the White House). If that watchfulness on the part of the international community, this insistent demand from outside the country that officials of the former government who committed crimes be held accountable, turns out to be so essential it is because of a bizarre moral sickness that infects transitions to democracy in our time. I have seen the situation in my own Chile and again in the case of the former Yugoslavia. And Cambodia. And Romania. And the Philippines. And in far too many other unfortunate lands across the globe as new leaders attempt to usher in an era of peace and stability.

It is members of the new government, often the very people who led the resistance against the dictatorship, who are all too often the ones who preach a selective amnesia, asking their citizens to focus on the future and not on what happened yesterday. Investigating the horror, they say, dragging up old crimes, putting former officials on trial, only diverts attention from the most urgent task at hand, the primary goal of national reconciliation. In the case of Chile, the newly elected democratic leaders failed to realize that this mythic coming together of a fractured nation could not possibly be attained by ignoring the pain of the past. They did not realize that the cost of allowing the former ruler and his followers utter impunity led to the erosion of the rule of law and the mortgaging of our ethical future. If a judge in Spain—

Ariel Dorfman

with the concurrence of the British court system—had not embarrassed us into prosecuting Pinochet, he would still be giving self-congratulatory speeches in the Senate. In his case, as in the ongoing trial of Milosevic, it is clear that the increasing authority and vigilance of international tribunals help rather than hinder the search for justice at the local and national levels.

The fact that Pinochet finally was able to avoid prosecution due to spurious health reasons has not, in the year that has followed, deterred this advance towards accountability at a global level. The two war crimes tribunals—for the former Yugoslavia and Rwanda—are functioning well, as is the special tribunal for Sierra Leone. Enough countries have ratified the Rome Statute of the International Criminal Court so that a discussion of how it will function and who will serve on it is already in the offing. The very circumstance that it will soon start to operate will make future Pinochets and past Milosevics even more wary. As we head into a world riddled by the dilemmas posed by the terrorist attacks of September 11, 2001, and the U.S. response to them, we will be seeing, I believe, a recrudescence of violations against the rights of people. Terror exercised by rulers against their own people will be overlooked—as in Chechnya and Pakistan, Turkey and Tibet—due to the obsessive American need to focus on that other war, the "war against terrorism," or the accompanying American lack of interest in any region (such as Latin America or Africa) that does not seem essential to that campaign.

Not to mention those major human rights violators in nations like Iraq and North Korea who have been defined as so outside the American orbit of influence that no incentive exists any longer to ease up on the terrible way their own subjects are treated. In short, we seem to be more in need than ever of international institutions accepted by all parties and countries that can hear those crimes against humanity that national courts cannot or will not attend to. It is disheartening, though not unexpected, that the world's only superpower opposes such an instance and will not recognize its rulings.

Indeed, if such a tribunal had been in place, the whole Pinochet affair might not have happened at all: Chile would have had to give its former dictator up if it was not willing or able to try him. But Chile would not have felt (as Serbia does, with some justification) that there is a double standard at work here. Only the war criminals from weak nations are put on trial. If your country is big enough, you can get away with—say—Tianamen Square or mining the ports of Nicaragua. But of course that is one of the problems with the International Criminal Court: Besides the fact that it will be some time before such an institution is up and functioning, it remains to be seen whether its pronouncements will be accepted by all signatories. Meanwhile, it is encouraging that the Pinochet prosecution has become the model and inspiration for other actions.

Hissène Habré, for instance, the genocidal ruler of Chad, was living in pomp in nearby Senegal with the money he had stolen from his country until a group of Senagalese citizens, galvanized by the accomplishments of Garcés and Garzón, accused him of torture and murder, charges that were accepted by a Senegalese judge. When the "African Pinochet" (yes, that is what they called him) was freed by a superior tribunal—much in the way that a court in Chile finally found a way to exempt Pinochet from standing trial—the Belgians, who have steadfastly been proclaiming their right to judge former heads of state for crimes against humanity—stepped in and demanded Habré's extradition, a case that is still being argued. The Belgians are also seeking to put Ariel Sharon on trial for his participation in the 1982 Shabra and Shatila massacres in Lebanon. There have, naturally, also been setbacks—like the UN withdrawal from the Cambodian courts that were supposed to judge the lethal Khmer Rouge cadres, because there was no guarantee of independence; or the refusal of each and every Argentine government to extradite some of its worse human rights abusers; or the ruling by the International Court of Justice in The Hague (the UN's official judicial arm) that Belgium's arrest warrant against Yerodia Ndomabasi, the former foreign minister of the Democratic Republic of Congo, for genocide was illegal. On other fronts, however, progress is being made: Kissinger cancels a trip to Brazil because Judge Garzón (yes, he's still at it, going strong) is threatening to have him arrested for his role in installing the Chilean dictatorship in 1973; the former governor of East Timor is arraigned for having arranged the massacre of thousands during the last months of Indonesian occupation of that island; an American judge rules that Shell can be held responsible and put on trial for its collusion with the Nigerian government in the death of poet and activist Ken Saro-Wiwa and others. I am not suggesting that these actions and so many others should be directly attributed to the extradition trial of General Pinochet, but historians may well argue many centuries from now that his prosecution, because of its prominence and the precedent it established of universal jurisprudence, indeed constituted a turning point.

We can only surmise whether the defeat of Pinochet expresses a deep change in the moral climate, similar to what happened in the not-so-distant past when the slavery that seemed natural to most of the planet's elite became, in a matter of decades, absolutely abhorrent. There was a time when working eighty hours a week was not deemed unreasonable, when child labor was considered the lot of every poverty-stricken newborn baby, when a woman was automatically deemed inferior and voiceless—and we can pinpoint, in all these cases, certain major symbolic events that signaled a shift in the consensus of what was and was not permissible. Perhaps we are now on the verge of a similar transformation, the ability to imagine a world where rulers who plunder and kill their own populations are invariably supposed to receive some form of retribution. That is, at any rate my prediction: that the despots of today or maybe of the day after tomorrow will look into the cracked mirror of

Ariel Dorfman

Milosevic and into the murderous and hunted eyes of Pinochet and see, once and for all, their future.

But wait—didn't Pinochet finally get off? Isn't there a counter-lesson in that? Won't my hypothetical genocidal murderer say to himself, "I can always make believe I was crazy, I can always hang on until I am so senile that it is senseless to try to judge me at all."[5]

So—what is the final meaning of Pinochet? How will his story be interpreted many years from now? Isn't that the ultimate test of where his journey has taken him and us?

Let me hazard a prophecy: Of all the battles of his interminable life, the one that the General can no longer hope to win is the battle for the way in which he will be remembered beyond his death, how the hard syllables that form his name—Pi-no-chet--will endure and become solidified in tomorrow's vocabulary. The General has lost, I believe, the battle for control of the language of the future.

During most of my adult life, as I could not restrain what Pinochet himself was doing to me and my loved ones, I was fascinated by the possibility that perhaps we could, in some way, determine at least how the word *Pinochet* would be transmitted to the future. I was so haunted by the desire to foretell history's judgment that in one of my novels I conjectured that, thirty thousand years from now, in the mythical country of Tsil (as I suggested Chile might be known someday) children would insult their rivals by calling them "Pinchot," the

name of a particularly treacherous dragon in a caution-
ary fairy tale that parents in that faraway tomorrowland
would presumably tell their offspring. And yet, even
while I was merrily prognosticating Pinochet as an
expletive for generations to come, I was aware that in
the duel for a place in the common tongue of our time,
he was, in fact, carrying and conveying an import which
was rather less to my liking. Pinochet was not only
being associated with sudden military takeovers (such
as in the usage *Pinochetazo*), but with the iron fist supposedly needed to force an underdeveloped country into
accepting an economic model which would drag it,
kicking and quite literally screaming, into modernity
and progress. How often would I not hear in my travels
of exile the admiring and admonitory phrase: "What
this country needs is a Pinochet!" Meaning: This sad
land needs a real macho who will put potential troublemakers in their place. Yes, I thought, and terrorize them
so they will not offer resistance to the shock therapy
decreed by the global system as a precondition for foreign investment and FMI loans.

This ambiguous incarnation of Pinochet as both
bogeyman and paragon to be imitated far and wide did
not vanish, as I had hoped, when Chile returned, in
1990, to an uncertain and restricted democracy. Not
only was Pinochet held over our heads as a threat of
what might transpire if we ever tried to question the
prevailing system, but he was now being glorified by
other societies that were also undergoing their own tur-

bulent transitions to democracy. Russians of all sorts—and not only extreme nationalists—could be heard proclaiming that a "Soviet Pinochet" was imperative in their land, not to mention the great Vaclav Havel's vice premier Valtr Komarek who, in a visit to Chile, praised Pinochet as a "great personality" and an "original leader" whose economic model the Czechs would do well to emulate.

So both the man and that word, *Pinochet*, in spite of a worldwide campaign by the human rights community, managed to escape a connotation that was unequivocally negative. Overlapping and often superseding the image of the bloodthirsty and callous dictator was Pinochet as noble father figure to all those infantile inhabitants of a land who do not know what's good for them and require discipline. A modernizer, even a liberator, one who is not afraid to spill some blood in order, as Kissinger once infamously remarked, to save a nation from its own irresponsibility. A *warning* signal: that is what, up until the moment when he was arrested in England, Pinochet had come to symbolize to millions around the globe. Warning rebels not to dream of subversions and alternative versions of humanity, warning the poor about the dire consequences of being too unruly or libertarian or lazy or demanding.

The events of the last four years have, however, drastically reconfigured the semantics of Pinochet. His detention, trials and public abasement have led to an extraordinary transformation of that word *warning*, resignifying it: It is now the petty and grand tyrants of the world who, instead of their subjects, are filled with fear at the thought of Pinochet.

I would have to be more of an optimist than the history of the past century warrants to convince myself that Pinochet's example will instantaneously stay the hand of those who, encouraged by their governments to feel invulnerable, commit crimes against humanity and then shrug their shoulders, walk away from that pain smoking a cigarette or popping some candy into their mouth. But that image of Pinochet stripped of his immunity and arrested by Scotland Yard and then vilified by the courts in his own native Chile, must have infiltrated some part of the brain of those men, creeping into their eyes and sinews to remind them of the ominous destiny that could await them. And I also like to think of my friends—or at least some of them, one of them—in the solitary moment before he died, promising himself that the future holds some possible measure of justice, I like to imagine my friends murmuring to themselves that perhaps they are not eternally condemned to be victims perpetually forgotten, I like to think that they may have been right.

If human rights abuses will not cease because of the General's exemplary punishment, a subtle displacement has nevertheless been validated in the way in which the world imagines power and equality and memory.

For decades, I was ashamed that Chile had unfortunately given humanity the word as well as the person Pinochet.

Who would have thought that this word would end up being instead a legacy of ours to the planet, fervently notifying every child who is born on this earth that he must never, under no circumstance whatsoever, not ever, be a Pinochet.

Or better still, I imagine the children of the future, thousands of years hence, playing in a meadow or a playground.

And then one of them does or says something that warrants a reproach, an insult, a hideous slur, from the other one, who shouts out: "Oh, don't be a Pinochet."

"Pinochet?" answers the other. "Pinochet? Who's that?"

Pinochet?

Who in hell is Pinochet?

SOME FINAL WORDS IN THE GUISE
OF AN ACKNOWLEDGMENT

BEFORE I GET TO QUENO, let me start with the others.

This book would not exist if it had not been for my editor and friend at Seven Stories Press, Dan Simon, who convinced me that the General's never-ending trial was crying out for this sort of narration and then furthermore prodded me into writing something entirely different from what I had till then been writing rather extensively on the matter, challenging me to go ever further. Thanks to my editors at *El Pais* in Madrid, where Joaquín Estefanía and María Cordón helped to publish over twenty op-eds about the Pinochet case as it developed over three years. And a similar debt of gratitude needs to be expressed to the team at the *Los Angeles Times*, led by the remarkable Bob Berger (whose recent retirement as op-ed editor so many of us have had to lament). And I must add other editors who shepherded material that was later reworked in this book: Gerry Marzerati at *Harper's Magazine*, Kathleen Cahill at the *Washington Post*'s *Outlook* section, Matthew Rothschild at *The Progressive* and a host of others at London papers—Adrian Hamilton at *The Independent* and Mike Holland at *The Observer* and still others at the *Guardian* and the *Evening Standard*—and Michel Kajman at *Le Monde* and my friends at the *Frankfurter Algemeine Zeitung* in Germany and at *De Groene* and the *Volkskrant* in Holland.

And I also feel grateful for the support of my agents, Jin Auh and Raquel de la Concha, and for the invaluable help of Jennifer Prather, my faithful assistant who labored for hours retrieving material from the web and typing out notes. And what book of mine could be complete without remembering Angélica, my primary reader, and Rodrigo and Joaquín and Melissa and Isabella?

But it is to someone else I need to turn if the reader wants to know how a book like this is born.

When I decided that I did, in fact, need to revisit the story of General Pinochet and the terror that we have been trying to exorcise, I almost immediately—perhaps five minutes after the decision—sat down and wrote an e-mail to a friend in Chile. You know where it says "Subject" on an e-mail, up there under the address? Well, that's where I wrote the words "Help, Queno."

Queno is Eugenio Ahumada, perhaps my oldest friend in this world outside my parents—and I will say no more about the ties that bind us, but rather about the ties that bind him to the quest for the truth. During the years of the dictatorship, Queno was one of the archivists at the primary human rights organizations in Chile, first at the

Comité Pro Paz and then, when Pinochet shut down that ecumenical organization, at the Vicaría de la Solidaridad, set up by the Catholic Church in Chile to deal with the defense of the victims during the General's years of misrule. It is for someone else to tell the story of the archives of the Vicaría—the heart of any organization that fights injustice is its capacity to remember and those rooms full of files and documents were in the center of the struggle for memory. It was there that every accusation was recorded and catalogued. Chile's secret history was collected and recollected. The pain, yes, and the hope were registered. It was there that Queno received, at his desk, the news that his fellow archivist José Manuel Parada had been abducted by the Chilean secret police, violently snatched on the street as he was leaving his son at school, there that Queno learned two days later that José Manuel had been found in a ditch on the outskirts of Santiago, José Manuel in that ditch with his throat slit. Without those archives, there would have been no lawsuits against Pinochet, no detailed charges by the relatives, no Truth and Reconciliation Commission or Report, no material for the lawyers abroad to quote from, no articles by journalists telling Chile's story, no trial and, of course, no book like this one. Queno was only one of many unsung heroes, only one of those who, every day for years and years, sat down to make sure that all the horror and all of the resistance would be remembered. He could not have done it, along with his fellow workers at the human rights organizations, if hundreds and eventually thousands of others had not also contributed. So when I acknowledge him I am also recognizing all those anonymous and unnamed citizens of my country and so many others abroad who stubbornly persisted in the day-to-day task of memory, the impossible task of *la memoria olvidada*. They are the ones who made this book possible.

Oh yes. A few minutes after my request for aid from Queno, I got back an answer. Generally, Queno's responses are full of jokes and word games, obscure and convoluted references to our past escapades and to his children's many wondrous doings in the ruins (of Pompeii) and to musicals (like *Kiss Me, Kate*) and pop songs (he's an expert) and to movies (he writes film reviews on the web). This time all he said was: What do you want, bro?

Help, Queno. As usual. And you gave it. As usual. And not only to me.

Gracias, hermano.

NOTES

1. The latter was one of the reasons why the Argentine military thought they could count on Washington's neutrality when they invaded the Malvinas in 1982. The Americans instead stuck with their British NATO ally—and it is now coming out that Pinochet secretly aided that war effort against his Argentine neighbor. This is one reason why Thatcher is demanding that Westminster free the man who was crucial to her winning that battle in the South Atlantic and the subsequent general elections. How history twists and turns!

2. Thanks to Geoffrey Robertson, in whose book *Crimes Against Humanity: The Struggle for Global Justice* (New York: The New Press, 2000), I first read about these specific cases. The longer version I reproduce here is translated from Judge Baltasar Garzón's indictment as reproduced by the FASIC Foundation in Chile.

3. I thank Carmen Hertz for having sent me a facsimile of this letter. I had read its contents before (on a Web site), but to see the handwriting of Carlos right there, to feel the immediate intimacy of his hands writing to Carmen and writing also to us, those of us who in the future

remember him and have become in some way the guardians of his memory, to have been able to share that closeness turned out to be a gratifying experience in the midst of the pain that this book has wreaked upon me in ways I could not have foretold.

4   And even had something of a political career, eventually becoming the minister-spokesperson of the government of Eduardo Frei Ruiz Tagle, Eugenio's very own cousin.

5   Exactly one year later, in July 2002, when this book was going to press, the news arrives that five judges of the Supreme Court, by a vote of 4 to 1, have once and for all dismissed the case against Pinochet due to the irreversible deterioration of his mental faculties. This shameful capitulation of the judicial system was followed a few days later by the farce of the former dictator resigning, for the good of the fatherland, from his post of Senator-for-Life, though, of course, he kept his immunity as ex-president, his security detail, and his salary. In a letter which the "mentally ill patient" personally wrote, he defends with considerable acumen and rationality his government and his historical conduct. This grotesque spectacle was accompanied by his public statements of "I am not crazy." If the announcements by the government that "justice was done," have not transformed us into the laughing-stock of the world, it is only because some time ago the world had already lost any hope that the promise trumpeted when Pinochet returned to Chile would be honored.

FURTHER READING

Geoffrey Robertson. *Crimes Against Humanity: The Struggle for Global Justice* (New York: The New Press, 2000).

An excellent overview of this subject by one of the great human rights lawyers. It has been an indispensable text as I wrote this book.

William F. Schulz. *In Our Own Best Interest: How Defending Human Rights Benefits Us All* (Boston: Beacon Press, 2001).

For those who want to deepen their knowledge about the struggle for human rights in our time, by the executive director of the American section of Amnesty International.

Hugh O'Shaughnessy. *Pinochet: The Politics of Torture* (New York: New York University Press, 2000).

A first-rate introduction to the life and times of *el General*.

Patricia Verdugo. *Chile, Pinochet, and the Caravan of Death* (Miami, Florida: North-South Center Press, University of Miami, 2001).

Finally, the English translation of the classic *Los Zarpazos del Puma*, the definitive account of the Caravan of Death.

Pamela Constable and Arturo Valenzuela. *A Nation of Enemies, Chile Under Pinochet* (New York: Norton, 1991).

Published just after democracy returned to Chile, the reader can find here an even-handed account of the Pinochet regime.

Joseph Collins and John Lear. *Chile's Free-Market Miracle: A Second Look* (Oakland: A Food First Book, 1995).

Examines Pinochet's economic policies—a topic I barely had time to delve into.

AND FOR THOSE WHO KNOW SOME SPANISH:

Julio Scherer García. *Pinochet: Vivir Matando* (Mexico: Aguilar, 2000).

One of Latin America's best journalists brings us many extraordinary stories about Pinochet, his victims and the men and women who resisted his rule.

Raquel Correa and Elizabeth Subercaseaux. *Ego Sum Pinochet* (Santiago de Chile: Zig-Zag, 1989).

These two Chilean journalists interviewed Pinochet and extracted from him some amazing and self-revealing words.

Informe Rettig. *Informe de la Comisión de Verdad y Reconciliación, 1991.*

The most important human rights document in Chilean history: the two-volume, almost 900-page *Chilean Truth and Reconciliation Report.*

Rafael Otano. *Crónica de la Transición*, (Santiago de Chile: Planeta, 1995).

The best blow-by-blow account of Chile's transition to democracy.

Mónica González. *La Conjura* (Santiago de Chile: Ediciones B, 2000).

An indispensable book for those who want to find out everything about how Allende was overthrown and Pinochet's real role in that military coup d'état.

ABOUT THE AUTHOR

A "literary grandmaster" (*Time*) whose work constantly reveals how power and identity intersect, ARIEL DORFMAN has been hailed by the *Washington Post* as a "world novelist of the first order" and by *Newsweek* as "one of the greatest Latin American novelists." Dorfman, a Chilean exile since Pinochet's 1973 coup, which is the springboard for this book, has spent his life exploring the reality and dreams of the many Americas in Spanish and English. His works, translated into more than thirty languages, include the acclaimed memoir, *Heading South, Looking North*, and the novels *Widows*, *Konfidenz*, *Blake's Therapy*, and *The Nanny and the Iceberg*. Many of Dorfman's books are available in both English- and Spanish-language editions from Seven Stories Press. His plays have been performed in over one hundred countries, and his *Death and the Maiden* was made into a film by Roman Polanski. His latest plays are *Purgatory* and *Voices from Beyond the Dark: The Speak Truth to Power Play*. He has just published *In Case of Fire in a Foreign Land*, a book of poems. The recipient of many international awards, Dorfman contributes to major newspapers worldwide. He is a distinguished professor at Duke University and lives with his wife, Angelica, in Durham, North Carolina.

Ariel Dorfman's multimedia website:
http://adorfman.duke.edu

ABOUT SEVEN STORIES PRESS

Seven Stories Press is an independent book publisher based in New York City, with distribution throughout the United States, Canada, England, and Australia. We publish works of the imagination by such writers as Nelson Algren, Octavia E. Butler, Assia Djebar, Ariel Dorfman, Lee Stringer, and Kurt Vonnegut, to name a few, together with political titles by voices of conscience, including the Boston Women's Health Book Collective, Noam Chomsky, Ralph Nader, Gary Null, Project Censored, Barbara Seaman, Gary Webb, and Howard Zinn, among many others. Our books appear in hardcover, paperback, pamphlet, and e-book formats, in English and in Spanish. We believe publishers have a special responsibility to defend free speech and human rights wherever we can.

For more information about us, visit our Web site at www.sevenstories.com or write for a free catalogue to Seven Stories Press, 140 Watts Street, New York, NY 10013.

ABOUT OPEN MEDIA PAMPHLETS AND BOOKS

Open Media is a movement-oriented publishing project committed to the vision of "one world in which many worlds fit"—a world with social justice, democracy, and human rights for all people. Founded during wartime in 1991, Open Media has a ten year history of producing critically acclaimed and best-selling books and pamphlets that address our most urgent political and social issues.

Before and after September 11, Open Media has produced an array of anti-war works that focus on terrorism, "rogue states," U.S. propaganda, militarism, and the implications of U.S. foreign and domestic policies on human rights and civil liberties. These titles include:

9-11 by Noam Chomsky

Acts of Aggression: Policing "Rogue" States by Noam Chomsky with Edward W. Said

Bin Laden, Islam, and America's New "War on Terrorism" by As`ad AbuKhalil

Islands of Resistance: Puerto Rico, Vieques, and U.S. Policy by Mario Murillo

Israel/Palestine: How to End the 1948 War by Tanya Reinhart

Media Control: The Spectacular Achievements of Propaganda by Noam Chomsky

Propaganda, Inc. by Nancy Snow

Secret Trials and Executions by Barbara Olshansky

Sent by Earth by Alice Walker

Silencing Political Dissent by Nancy Chang

Terrorism: Theirs and Ours by Eqbal Ahmad

Terrorism and War by Howard Zinn

The Umbrella of U.S. Power by Noam Chomsky

Weapons in Space by Karl Grossman

Visit the Seven Stories Press web site for updated information and a complete list of all available Open Media books and pamphlets.

openmedia@sevenstories.com | www.sevenstories.com

ALSO BY ARIEL DORFMAN

FROM SEVEN STORIES PRESS

Blake's Therapy

Terapia (SIETE CUENTOS EDITORIAL)

Rumbo al sur, deseando el norte: Un romance en dos lenguas (SIETE CUENTOS EDITORIAL)

La muerte y la doncella (SIETE CUENTOS EDITORIAL)

Widows

The Nanny and the Iceberg (forthcoming)

FROM PENGUIN BOOKS

Death and the Maiden

Heading South, Looking North: A Bilingual Journey

The Empire's Old Clothes

FROM NICK HERN BOOKS

The Resistance Trilogy: Collected Plays

FROM DUKE UNIVERSITY PRESS

In Case of Fire in a Foreign Land: New and Collected Poems in Two Languages

Some Write to the Future: Essays on the Contemporary Latin American Novel

FROM DALKEY ARCHIVE PRESS

Konfidenz (forthcoming)